A Chronicle of Modern Sunlight

The story of what happened to the Rhodesians

W. G. Eaton

A Chronicle of Modern Sunlight

First published in the United States of America 1996 by:

InnoVision
555 Santa Alicia Dr.
Rohnert Park, CA 94928-3213

Library of Congress Cataloguing in Publication Data

Eaton, W.G.
A Chronicle of Modern Sunlight
1 Rhodesia, 2 Africa, 3 Migration, 4 Survey
Library of Congress Catalog Card No. 96-94398
ISBN 0-9652686-5-9 968.910

Printed in the USA.

The cover design shows the ancient ruins of Zimbabwe. Artwork supplied by Vic MacKenzie

10 9 8 7 6 5 4 3 2 1

Contents

Main Findings

Background and Migration

Education Patterns

Employment Patterns

Demographics

Opinions and Attitudes

And that's the way it was

Foreword and Thanks

I conceived this project in 1993. It had been at the back of my mind for several years. I had lived in Rhodesia (as it then was) from 1968-1979 and played a small and undistinguished role in the war that led to the establishment of Zimbabwe.

I moved to South Africa and then later to the USA. I often wondered what had happened to a very energetic and proud community of Rhodesians who had scattered throughout the world. Although there were only about 250 000 white Rhodesians and probably 50 - 100,000 remain in Zimbabwe this small nation made a major impact on the world political scene in the sixties and seventies when UDI was in full swing. Although there were some 5 million black Rhodesians (now 7 million Zimbabweans) I have concentrated this study on the white Rhodesians as the great majority of our black compatriots remained in Zimbabwe and thus did not take part in the worldwide Diaspora.

What had happened to the small tribe that held the whole world at bay for some 15 years? As Rhodesia became Zimbabwe some 15 years ago I realized that if history was to have some record of the migration of this small tribe something had to be done soon. I decided to find out what had happened. By profession I am a market researcher and so possessed the tools to carry out a suitable survey.

How the study was conducted

Early in 1994 I started to plan my project. I wrote to all the Rhodesian Associations I could locate asking for cooperation and input. All, with one exception, were extremely helpful and offered full support. At this time I made contact with Professor Cheater in New Zealand who was a major help in both design and subsequent analysis. With her input I continued with the questionnaire design stage and by early 1995 I was ready to launch.

The obvious difficulty lies in contacting approximately 200 000 people scattered in many countries of the world where they form a fraction of the overall population. In such circumstances mail is the only solution. Luckily there are organizations of ex-Rhodesians in several countries, most of which have a newsletter and a worldwide magazine called "Rhodesians Worldwide" is published from the United Kingdom.

The first batch of questionnaires was inserted in "Contact" (the newsletter of the Rhodesian Association-USA) by Vic MacKenzie early in 1995. This magazine circulates to about 250 Rhodesians in the USA. From the answers received the questionnaire was slightly amended before being reprinted for the rest of the world.

In total some 5000 questionnaires were printed. In the USA my parents helped fold and collate all the questionnaires of which about 4500 were sent out. "Rhodesians Worldwide" in the United Kingdom distributed about 2500 worldwide. The Rhodesian Air Force Association distributed several hundred to their members around the world from their United Kingdom base. Another 2000 was sent to South Africa for distribution but, due to customs delays, missed the overall South African mailing by the Rhodesian Association of South Africa (RASA and the Flame

Lily Foundation). About 1000 were distributed in the main regional newsletter from Pretoria that went to all regions with the exceptions of Durban and Cape Town. As many replies were received from those cities, from the Rhodesians Worldwide mailing the omission is considered minimal.

In Australia the Rhodesian Association of Western Australia mailed out questionnaires. Mike Hambrook personally distributed questionnaires at the Anzac day parade in Sydney (a Rhodesian contingent marches in the procession) and attracted much attention.

In Canada the Rhodesian Association of Ontario distributed questionnaires. In New Zealand Professor Cheater and Rhodesians Worldwide (NZ) helped distribute questionnaires to Rhodesians there. It was a great feeling to get such cooperation from so many people and organizations. The only organization that refused help was the BSAP Regimental Association who told me exactly where to insert my survey (although many members individually completed questionnaires).

Overall there was a substantial worldwide distribution to the main countries of Rhodesian settlement. Recipients were asked to photocopy questionnaires and pass them to Rhodesian acquaintances who had not received them. This resulted in over 200 extra responses and helped give statistical balance to the survey as this group's responses are often different to the members of Rhodesian Associations. Replies came from Andorra, France, Hong Kong, Japan, Indonesia, Malta, Norway, Oman, Peru, Portugal, Spain, Russia, Saudi Arabia, and several other countries out of the mainstream of Rhodesian settlement.

There were some amusing sidelights. While researching the cheapest way to air freight the questionnaires around the world, I discovered that North West Airlines was offering a winter special on flights to Europe from the USA. A quick calculator exercise revealed that two tourist tickets to the United Kingdom were cheaper than the regular air freight cost. Consequently my daughter and I arrived at San Francisco airport with personal luggage consisting of 90 kg. of questionnaires and a small bag of clothing and personal effects between us. To their credit the airline officials accepted my three "personal luggage" crates of questionnaires without query.

In total over 1460 questionnaires were received. Most were returned by mail but about 5% were returned by fax and a handful by Internet Email. This represents a response of level of just under 30% which is excellent, particularly when the circumstances of some respondents are considered - over 20% are aged over 70 and many had lost assets or income to such an extent that mailing an extra letter was a hardship. Many of this group appeared to suffer from arthritic problems but struggled to complete the text answers despite their handicaps (the oldest respondent was over 90). In almost all cases there was a fierce pride and a plea to tell the world what the Rhodesians had accomplished in the country's 90 years of existence.

Overall I had never anticipated such a response (I expected about 4-500, based on previous experience). As I was entering the entire data by myself, in my spare time, my spare room took on the appearance of a stationery warehouse and it took considerably longer than anticipated (data entry required about 3,2 million keystrokes). It is a measure of the pride Rhodesians felt for their country that created such a response. People who had left the country over 40 years ago still belonged to the various associations and returned questionnaires. I felt very humble.

This is the story of a small tribe of Europeans who created a modern country from African bush, then lost it and their subsequent wanderings. The title indicates one of my favourite modern authors and one of the main feelings of loss, experienced by the Rhodesians.

Stats and all that stuff

All figures are given in percentages (except where stated) and are based on the total sample size of 1460 respondents. As in all surveys there is a measure of sampling error. In this case the confidence interval does not exceed 3.7% at the 50% level. What this means is that if the difference between two figures is greater than 3.7% the difference is a genuine one. It may also be genuine if the figure is less, depending on the percentage values.

The necessary difference will be larger where smaller sub-samples are concerned. For example if comparing answers between the Australian respondents and the UK respondents the equation must be based on the Australian sample size (176) and the UK sample size (466). Fortunately the program used does this automatically and saves much brain power. Where percentages approach the end of the scale e.g., 90% or 10% the confidence interval is less. In almost all cases I have not commented on differences that do not meet or exceed the confidence interval.

Two other terms are used. Confidence level is set at 95%. This is statistical convention and means that the data will be correct 95% of the time (i.e., random error will occur 5% of the time).

The other term is "significant" which is mentioned frequently. In statistics this has a specific meaning. It does not necessarily mean "important" in the usual sense. It means that the data meets the criteria for confidence intervals and confidence levels mentioned above and so can be called "significantly" different to the other data.

Differences between various groups of figures are not mentioned in this report unless they meet the tests of significance (with a few exceptions noted in the text).

For those interested in the full data set, bound paper copies are available. A word of warning - the paper report is almost 5 cm. thick and weighs 2 kg. The disk containing the full data set and explanations (zipped) is available in IBM format only. Internet users can also download the files, at no charge, from the Rhodesian Page on the Internet at:

http://scorpion.cowan.edu.au/~rwebb/index.html

Full details and order forms are in the back of this report.

Technical Notes

The questionnaires were entered into an IBM PC by the data capture clerk (myself). The data file totalled about 3.2 MB. The program used was The Survey System™ - a program designed specifically for analyzing questionnaire data. The perceptual maps were created by NCSS™ (Number Cruncher Statistical System). Most charts were created by Harvard Graphics™ and the report was written in Word for Windows™.

Acknowledgments

I received considerable help from many sources and note some of those below. If I have omitted anyone I apologize - it was a sin of omission rather than commission. Thanks to the following who helped me in many ways with guidance, input or logistics.

People

Professor Angela Cheater, then of the University of Waikato, New Zealand for much guidance and acting as the New Zealand post box.
Mr. and Mrs. Ralph Gilbertson for logistical help in folding and packing questionnaires.
Mr. Mike Hambrook for distributing questionnaires in Australia and acting as the Australian post box.
My daughter (the South African post box).
My brother (the United Kingdom post box).
The people who sent donations to help with the project. Where possible I thanked them personally but many were anonymous.
All the many respondents who sent their best wishes.
My wife and family for allowing many hours of neglect as I slaved over a hot computer.

Organizations

Rhodesians Worldwide.
The Rhodesian Air Force Association.
The Rhodesian Association of the USA.
The Rhodesian Association of South Africa
The Flame Lily Foundation of Pretoria.
The Rhodesian Association of Ontario, Canada.
The Rhodesian Association of Western Australia.

Potted History for Outsiders

Rhodesia, as a modern state, began in 1890 with the arrival of the Pioneer Column, led by Frank Johnson and financed by Cecil Rhodes. They were searching for a fabled gold reef that was believed to be an extension of the Witwatersrand reef, which has never been located. It became a country ruled by the British South Africa Company and suffered 2 rebellions against its rule in 1893 and 1896. Almost 10% of the white population died in this early war of resistance by the native population. In 1923 the (white) electorate chose self determination in preference to incorporation with South Africa as an extra province. In 1953 it joined the Central African Federation with Northern Rhodesia (Zambia) and Nyasaland (Malawi). The Federation was dissolved in 1963 at the instigation of the British Government, caused largely by opposition from the black populations of the territories. The other two members became independent states within the next year. Despite its excellent record of development of a virgin African territory without foreign aid Rhodesia was refused the same option because it did not offer the vote to all citizens regardless of colour. Instead it possessed a limited franchise system, restricted by education and income, which effectively kept power in the hands of the whites. Its' supporters claimed that in time this would have lead to a majority black government. After several years of fruitless negotiation with the United Kingdom government, who showed bad faith on several occasions, Rhodesia decided to declare itself independent (UDI- unilateral declaration of independence). This occurred on 11 November 1965. It brought down the wrath of the United Kingdom, the USA, the United Nations and many other countries and organizations who imposed almost total prohibitions on dealings with Rhodesia.

Despite this, Rhodesia prospered in the late sixties, due in part to an intensive program of import replacement by local manufacture. Early attempts by African Nationalists to stage a guerrilla uprising were easily crushed by the Rhodesian Security Forces. The Nationalists retreated and began a clandestine long-term campaign to infiltrate the country from Zambia and Mozambique. Late in 1972 they restarted their "Chimurenga" (freedom) war that raged until 1980. It was a small scale war by world standards but it involved every Rhodesian family as growing military call-ups took men away from jobs and homes for increasing periods. The slowing of the world economy and the oil price shocks in the early seventies also hindered Rhodesia by lowering its export prices and hiking the costs of fuel imports. Many of the black residents of Rhodesia suffered from the disruption of the war, with vicious intimidation attempts by the guerrillas (and to a lesser extent by the Rhodesians). The war lasted longer than the second World War. Several attempts to obtain a negotiated peace were made but these failed. After much negotiation Britain took over interim administration of the country in 1979 and held elections which were widely considered to be rife with intimidation. These resulted in a massive victory for the Marxist leaning ZANU-PF under the leadership of Robert Mugabe. Mugabe has remained President of Zimbabwe ever since and most of the white Rhodesians left the country to settle elsewhere. This book chronicles their activities since then.

Due to strict exchange controls very few Rhodesians emigrated with adequate capital to start a new life. Until about 1975 families could take up to $Rh. 5000 (then about US$6000) out of the country with them. This was then lowered to $Rh. 1000 per family or $500 per single individual. When the new government took power it also limited the export of personal effects to: clothing, one lounge suite, one dining room suite per family and one bed per family member and a car to start a new life. Even personal possessions had to be owned for 2 years prior to emigration and cars had to be at least 4 years old before being exported. Proof, in the form of purchase receipts, was required before export permits were issued.

The Readers Digest Version

The first surprise is that there is no such thing as a typical Rhodesian and that each country of settlement has collected a different group of Rhodesians.

Over a third of the Rhodesians were born in the United Kingdom, slightly fewer in the country itself, and 15% in South Africa. The remainder were born in many other countries. Just over a quarter immigrated to pre-arranged employment and slightly fewer came with their parents, 10% came without employment and 3% were transferred by employers.

The average Rhodesian had spent 30 years in the country and left in 1980. Most have returned about 3 times, mainly to visit relatives but this is much higher among South African residents due to the proximity.

Almost half the Rhodesians settled in South Africa on leaving Rhodesia and about 30% in the United Kingdom, followed by Australia with 8% and other countries. Over half the South African group are now aged over 60 compared to 40% in the United Kingdom and only 14% in the USA.

A fair number have moved a second, and even third time. The main loser has been South Africa which lost 11% of the 49%. Most of these went either to the United Kingdom or Australia, although the United Kingdom also lost some settlers (mainly to Australia). The main reasons for leaving South Africa were the fear of impending black rule, the high level of violent crime and dislike of the Afrikaans ethos. The main reason for leaving Britain was the climate and the economy. As a result families were widely scattered with members in several countries.

A quarter of the sample claimed university or professional qualification in Rhodesia and 16% have gained similar qualifications since leaving. However this figure varies considerably by country from 8% in South Africa to 39% in the USA. This correlates highly with age - the younger respondents have studied more since leaving Rhodesia.

Only 16% of respondents have stayed in the same type of job and industry as they were in during their Rhodesians days. A similar proportion is now retired. In Canada respondents tended to stay in the same job type in a different industry but the reverse prevailed in Australia and New Zealand. US residents were more likely to make complete breaks with both industry and job types. Almost a quarter have changed both job type and industry.

It took the average Rhodesian 2½ months to find work, with the shortest period being 1¾ months in New Zealand and South Africa and up to 3.1 months in the United Kingdom and the USA. The same Rhodesian has changed jobs nearly 3 times since then and there is an inverse proportion - the longer it took to find the first job the more he or she was likely to change jobs.

A quarter each of the sample was civil servants and businessmen and 12% were professionals. Most civil servants and pensioners went to South Africa or the United Kingdom. Professionals were more likely to go the USA or the United Kingdom.

Only 5% are now in the civil service and almost a third are now pensioners. There has been a growth in self employment by both professionals and technical people.

On the agreement scales almost a quarter would return to live in Zimbabwe if possible but three quarters would return for a holiday. The highest degree of agreement was the 89% who are still proud to be called Rhodesians. Most, except the oldest group and residents of the United Kingdom believe they are now better off than in Rhodesian days. There is ambivalence about whether UDI was a success with a score of 2.9 out of 5. Technically educated people were much more in favour than professional people. Most respondents believe that Zimbabweans are worse off now than in the past

The average respondent is 57 years old with South Africans being the oldest at 61 and American residents the youngest at 48. Several respondents were in their nineties!

Almost two thirds are still with the same marital partner as they were in Rhodesia. This figure would be even higher if we excluded the high number of widows, especially in South Africa. The group with the highest divorce rate appears to be those who left Rhodesia as children and came of age in other countries.

Almost half the respondents held UK passports at birth but this dropped to 20% in Rhodesia and returned to the original level now. The "missing" 25% in Rhodesia held both Rhodesian and British passports. A similar process took place with South African passport holders. Most respondents now seem to have adopted the passport of their country of residence.

Over two thirds have managed to purchase either a house or an apartment. This is highest in Australia and New Zealand and lowest in the United Kingdom. Older respondents are more likely to own apartments than houses. Ownership rises directly with time since leaving Rhodesia.

Almost two thirds of respondents belong to Rhodesians Worldwide and almost a third to RASA/Flame Lily. The Rhodesian Christian Group has a very old age profile (over two thirds are over 60 and most live in South Africa). Sixteen percent of respondents belonged to no organization and received their questionnaires through the photocopying efforts of friends.

The main reason for leaving Rhodesia/Zimbabwe was rejection of majority rule by over a quarter of the respondents, linked with related fears such as education, future stability and employment. However 20% of the reasons were family related (often parents leaving to join younger children who had previously emigrated). The war itself rated only a 5% mention. Time of leaving made a difference with "black" and "majority rule" being quoted more by people who left from 75-79 and "communist", "education" and "government" being more common among those who left from 80-83. Economic and financial reasons were more important from 84-89 when the results of several years of socialist policies were becoming evident. Family reasons were strongest among South African residents.

Preferred destinations varied by decade with the USA being more popular in the 60's and 70's and new Zealand in the 90's. The United Kingdom was least popular in the 80's.

The longer a person had lived in Rhodesia - the later the date of departure on average. This reflects both loyalty to Rhodesia, the inability to move financial assets from the country and arrival of pensionable age in many cases.

Employment was the major motivator to move from the first country after Rhodesia, except in South Africa where dislike of South African policies, rising crime and impending black rule were major factors. Again there was substantial migration to regroup families.

Lifestyle, friends and the country are the major items people miss about Rhodesia. The major way of retaining this is by keeping in touch with Rhodesian friends.

The major problem experienced in their new land was culture shock at 30%. Surprisingly this was stronger than financial problems at 19% although, again, there were marked differences. Canadians felt most culture shock and financial problems were most in evidence in Australia. UK residents suffered more with employment and accommodation than others. Homesickness affected females and New Zealanders to a greater extent than anyone else. Twenty-two percent did not answer this question and 9% claimed no problems giving almost a third who seemed to have no problems worth mentioning.

Currently the major problem is financial - especially in the United Kingdom and South Africa. In South Africa much of this was related to pensions and exchange rates. Crime is still a major problem in South Africa and the USA. Climate is a problem in the United Kingdom and Canada and lack of friends in Australia.

The best liked aspects of the current country vary widely according to country. England rates highly for the beauty of the countryside, history, culture, health, consumer choice and travel opportunities. However it also has the highest level of "no likes". Australia rates highly for stability, opportunity, open politics and space. New Zealand also rates highly for space, the greenery and the friendly locals. The beauty, climate, family ties and the wild game are South Africa's main attractions. The USA rates highly for stability, opportunity and wide consumer choice.

The major dislike is climate - especially in the United Kingdom and Canada, and to a lesser extent, New Zealand. Politics is the second biggest dislike, especially in South Africa and Australia (despite it being a preference above). In South Africa the racial aspect was also a problem.

Parochial attitudes and litter are a problem in the United Kingdom. South Africans are considered brusque and rude and crime, bureaucracy and inefficiency remain major problems in that country. Crime is also a problem to US residents.

The quarter of the sample would return to Zimbabwe to live have many distinguishing characteristics from the others. They generally have less education or are more technically oriented with no further education since Rhodesian days. They have changed career paths and jobs more than most, returned to Zimbabwe more often and have little faith in the future of their current country (frequently South Africa). They are conspicuous non-owners of property and left Zimbabwe for educational reasons - mainly for their children. They have obviously not settled in their current country and have more dislikes than most, irrespective of the country settled.

Main Findings

Background and Migration

Where did the Rhodesians come from?

Surprisingly slightly more Rhodesians were born in the United Kingdom than in Rhodesia itself (although this not statistically significant - see introductory page on stats and all that). This stems partially from the country's original founding by the British South Africa Company, the promotion of immigration from Britain and the second world war when Rhodesia hosted an aircrew training scheme for the Royal Air Force. Many of these trainees returned after the war to settle. There was also substantial immigration of other British people, often disillusioned by post-war austerity in the United Kingdom and officially encouraged by the British government. There are very different age groups within this table. The oldest group was mainly born in the United Kingdom or Europe and, to a lesser extent, South Africa. The youngest group came from other African countries (usually after Independence there) or were born in Rhodesia itself reflecting the changing waves of immigration and the change from an immigrant receiving country to a more established, self-propagating one.

Where the Rhodesians came from

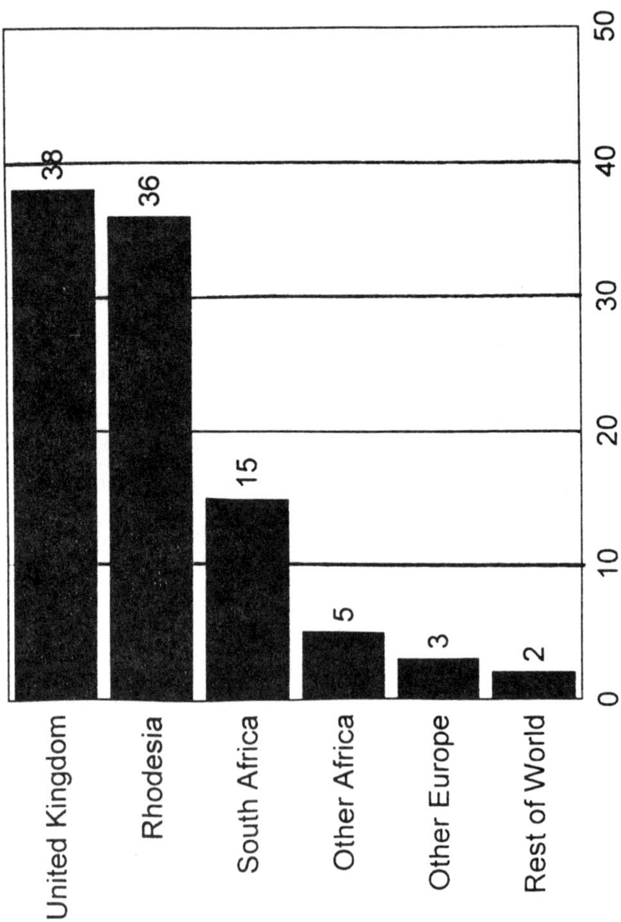

Where did they go?

	%
South Africa	49
United Kingdom	29
Australia	8
Canada	3
USA	3
New Zealand	2

Almost half the Rhodesians moved to South Africa first - far ahead of the United Kingdom at 29%. A higher proportion of those born in the United Kingdom and South Africa returned to their respective countries while those born in Rhodesia tended to avoid the United Kingdom.

Movement Patterns

Those who had lived longest in Rhodesia tended to move to South Africa but those with 11-30 years residence moved to the United Kingdom and those with under 10 years moved more to the USA. There were also differences according to year of departure. Those leaving before 1970 and after 1990 favoured New Zealand, those leaving from 75-79 favoured the United Kingdom and from 80-83 either South Africa or Australia.

Other differences emerged. More of those believing UDI to be a success went to South Africa while those believing it a failure went to Australia and the USA. This also reflected educational patterns with the less skilled going to South Africa, the technically trained to the United Kingdom and the professionals to the USA and other countries.

Where do they live now?

Judging by the countries of origin of the questionnaires and the assumption that about 200,000 Rhodesians left the country the following pattern of settlement is likely.

	%	No.
South Africa	38	75,000
United Kingdom	32	65,000
Australia	12	25,000
USA	6	10,000
Canada	3	7,000
New Zealand	3	5,000
Other Europe	1	3,000
Rest of World	1	6,000
Total		196,000

These figures are multiplied from the sample base to add to almost 200,000. They are subject to considerable uncertainty. Also the strength of the local Rhodesian Association and its mailing may have influenced the number of returns. Professor Cheater (who has studied the matter closely) is critical of this figure believing it to be too high in the light of her studies. She believes a much higher proportion (over 100,000) may still be resident in Zimbabwe. Another 1995 estimate in the London Sunday Times placed the level at 80,000. The current government in Zimbabwe does not generally reveal racial statistics so this cannot be fully verified. There are no other really reliable sources to verify or deny this. My personal experiences indicate at least one Rhodesian in each small town in northern California. Multiplication to a national level (a statistically dubious procedure) would indicate a figure of 10-12,000 Rhodesians in the USA. Unfortunately the US

Immigration and Naturalization Service records immigrants by country of birth making it impossible to count non native-born Rhodesians accurately.

Many Rhodesians returned to the country of their birth (mainly Britain and South Africa) but the highest proportion who live in the USA and Canada were born in Rhodesia itself.

There are considerable age variations in the pattern of migration. The oldest group moved mainly to South Africa, where 55% are aged over 60 the middle aged to Australia and the youngest groups to the USA or Canada (where the over 60's represent 14% and 30% of the group respectively). Conversely only 25% of South Africa's settlers are under 50 while almost two thirds of those in the USA are under 50. The United Kingdom received either the young or the old - but not so many middle aged. The diagram on the following page shows the very different age distribution in each country.

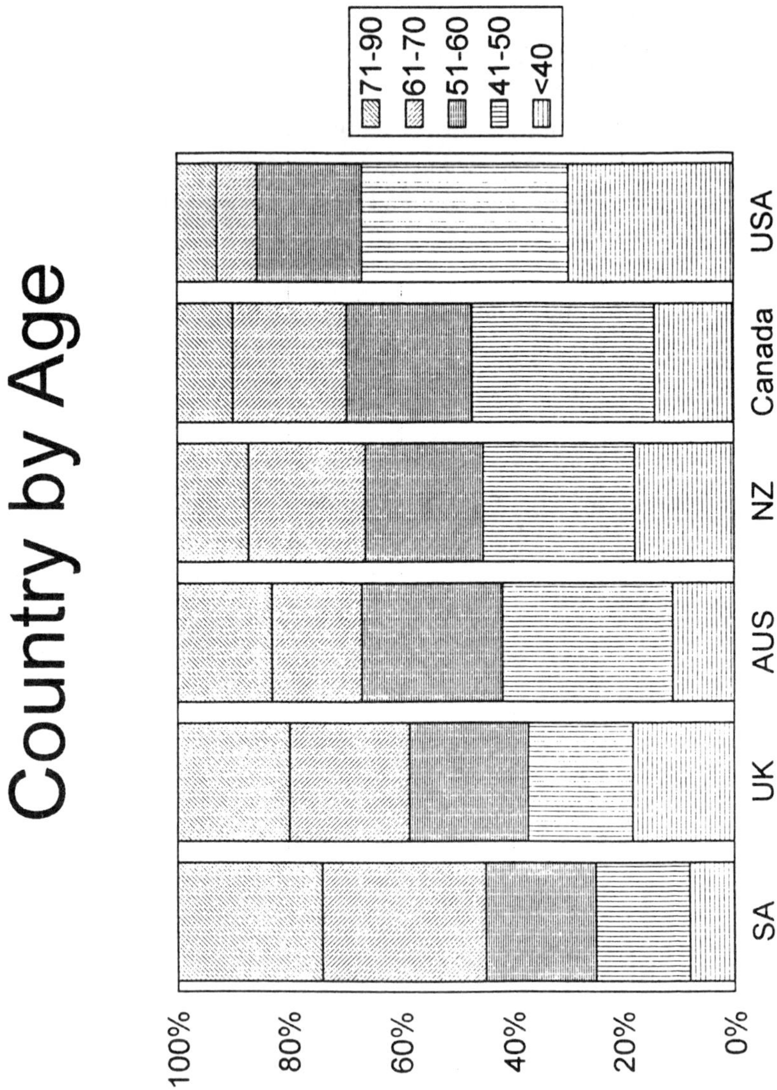
Country by Age
71-90
61-70
51-60
41-50
<40
100%
80%
60%
40%
20%
0%
SA
UK
AUS
NZ
Canada
USA

Number of years in current country

Average number of years 12

Given the mean departure date of 1980 to the survey date of 1995 (15 years) there is obviously substantial movement between countries to account for the missing 3 years.

Other Moves

A considerable number has made second (and even third or fourth) moves from their first choice to other countries.

Country	First Move	Live Now	Change
South Africa	49%	38	-11
United Kingdom	29	32	+3
Australia	8	12	+4
USA	3	6	+3
Canada	3	3	0
New Zealand	2	3	+1
Other Europe	2	1	-1
Other country	3	1	-2

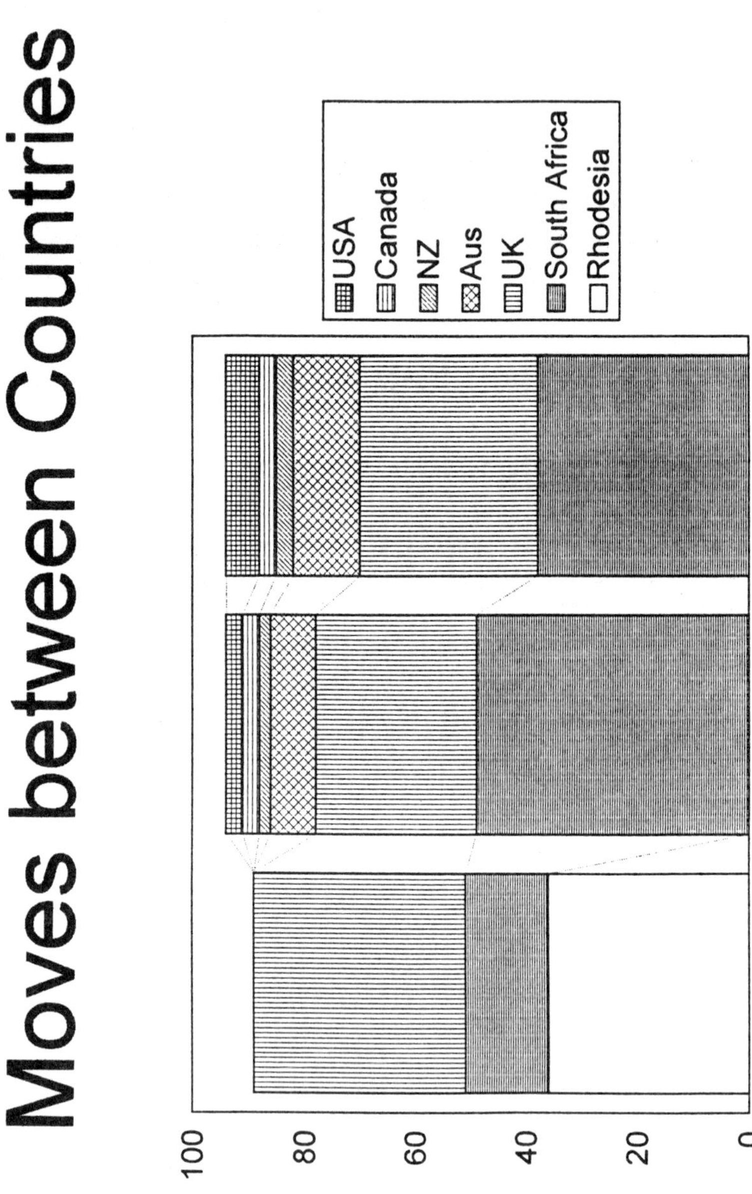
Moves between Countries
USA
Canada
NZ
Aus
UK
South Africa
Rhodesia
Birth
First Move
Now
100
80
60
40
20
0

South Africa has been the major loser in the second wave. This has been due to a sense of "déjà vu" and approaching black rule in South Africa or a dislike for the former South African government policies of apartheid. Most of these went either to the United Kingdom or Australia. However the traffic has not all been one way and a considerable number has left the United Kingdom for South Africa. The United Kingdom has also lost a considerable number to Australia. The losses in other countries have mainly been due to migratory contract workers. Many Rhodesians took lucrative but unpleasant jobs in the Middle East and other under-developed countries to recoup some of their losses in Rhodesia. After several years many returned to more Western countries with an improved capital base.

	Country moved from					
Country moved to	**SA**	**UK**	**Australia**	**NZ**	**Canada**	**USA**
SA	-11%	2			n	n
UK	7	+3	n		n	n
Aus	2	2	+4	n	n	n
NZ	1	n	n	+1	n	n
Can	1	n	n	n	+0.5	n
USA	2	1	n	n	n	+2

n = negligible

The table above shows the trend of secondary migration. The columns show the country moved from and the rows show the country moved to. For example 7% of the 49 % that settled in South Africa then moved to the United Kingdom, while 2% of the 29% that settled in the United Kingdom moved to South Africa. The + or - figures along the intersection of the row and the column show the total secondary migration to that country. Thus the -11% shows South Africa's net loss.

Younger respondents have moved to more countries than the older ones. In total 12% of the respondents have moved 3 or more times with the United Kingdom suffering most of the third moves from it.

		Current Residence					
Country of Birth		SA	UK	Australia	NZ	Canada	USA
United Kingdom	38%	29	53	41	26	22	18
Rhodesia	36	37	32	34	44	49	54
South Africa	15	24	8	14	13	12	12
Other Africa	5	5	4	6	3	6	4
Other Europe	3	2	2	3	6	5	3
Rest of World	2	2	2	2	13	4	6

The table above adds to 100% vertically in each column. In the left column 38% were born in the United Kingdom but in the shaded block of the third column 53% of the Rhodesians who live in the United Kingdom were born in the United Kingdom. It will be noted that born Rhodesians were more likely to head for the Americas and New Zealand than Rhodesians from other countries.

The table on the following page is the same as the one above except that the figures add to 100% horizontally. South Africa was the first preference for most Rhodesians, except those born in the United Kingdom. The shaded area shows that 29% of Rhodesians born in the United Kingdom now live in South Africa.

Birth Country		Current Residence						
		SA	UK	Australia	NZ	Canada	USA	Other
United K'dom	100	29	45	13	2	2	3	2
Rhodesia	100	38	28	11	3	5	9	3
South Africa	100	60	16	11	2	3	5	2
Other Africa	100	40	30	16	2	4	4	2
Other Europe	100	40	21	11	3	8	11	3
Rest of World	100	34	20	9	14	6	14	3

Overall Rhodesians born in either the United Kingdom or South Africa tended to return to the land of their birth. Born Rhodesians followed these destinations. Although born Rhodesians were the largest group to settle in South Africa, they did so to a smaller than their share of their total sample would indicate.

Family Distribution

	Self	**Parent**	**Sibling**	**Children**	**Grand children**
South Africa	38%	16	37	37	24
United Kingdom	32	14	27	24	11
Australia	3	3	8	12	6
New Zealand	3	1	2	3	1
Canada	3	1	2	3	2
USA	4	1	4	5	2
Zimbabwe	N/A	10	15	6	5

Although most of the relatives are in Britain or South Africa a higher proportion of children has moved to Australia, New Zealand, Canada or the USA. In general the younger the person (except grandchildren who are mainly still dependent) the further they have moved from the originating countries of South Africa and the United Kingdom. It is noteworthy that a fair number has children and or grandchildren who have remained in or returned to Zimbabwe.

Help to Settle

Ex Rhodesian friends	37%
Non Rhodesian friends/relatives	29
Rhodesian Association	2
Other charitable organization	1
No one	22

Although very few Rhodesians were helped to settle by a formal Rhodesian Association (Australia was the one exception where the figure reached 7%) there is a strong network of informal help from ex-Rhodesian friends in South Africa and Australia. United Kingdom and USA settlers were helped more by non Rhodesian friends - presumably relatives of Rhodesians of United Kingdom origin in the former case. This is backed up by the fact that those who had spent under 20 years in Rhodesia (i.e., immigrated from another country) received more help from non Rhodesian friends and relatives while those who had spent more than 40 years received most help from ex-Rhodesian friends. Other social organizations featured more strongly in Australia and New Zealand. The largest group to claim no help was received were those settling in South Africa.

The under 40 age group got more help from non Rhodesian friends (this is partially the USA group). The year of leaving Rhodesia also made a substantial difference. The later a person left the more likely they were to receive help from ex-Rhodesian friends which makes intuitive sense. Rhodesian Associations, especially RAWA (Rhodesian Association of Western Australia) were at their helping peak in the 80-83 period and other social organizations seemed to take over from 1984 onwards.

Years resident in Rhodesia

The average period of residence was 30 years with residents of South Africa staying longest (33 years) and US residents the least (25 years). It is noteworthy that length of residence increases in direct length to year of leaving. This may well reflect the greater attempts by long-established residents to come to terms with the new government. It may also reflect the fact that older residents were close to pension age and were financially unable to leave before reaching that point.

Emigration to Rhodesia

Own choice to pre-arranged job	26%
As child with parents	22
Own choice without pre-arranged job	10
Transferred by employer	3
Other	3
Born In Rhodesia	36

While 20% of the UK born Rhodesians emigrated without pre-arranged employment 9% of the South African born did so. However almost 6% of this group (twice the average) were transferred by employers. Those who went to pre-arranged jobs usually spent over 20 years in Rhodesia while those who went without employment spent under 20 years - partially reflecting the difficulties of overseas recruiting after UDI. The small proportion of other at 3% shows an interesting sex difference (2% male and 8% female) which is mainly explained by the preponderance of non-Rhodesian females marrying Rhodesian males and entering the country as spouses.

Most the technically or other educated people had immigrated with or without employment while a high proportion of the professionally trained people was locally born or had accompanied their parents.

Leaving Rhodesia

Child with parents	4%
Adult by own choice	96

Almost all left as adults but paradoxically a high proportion (12% compared to 4% overall) of those who left as children did so before 1970 but still remain interested enough to complete the questionnaire although they also form a high proportion of the group that does not belong to any Rhodesian group. Most of those who left as children (80%) were Rhodesian born.

Year of Leaving Rhodesia/Zimbabwe

Mean year 1980

The mean year of leaving corresponds exactly with Independence. Among the group that left prior to 1970 the mean year of leaving was 1963 - which marked the end of Federation and another watershed in Rhodesian history. It is again remarkable that a group that left a country over 30 years previously still retained enough links to complete a survey of this type, indicating a strong loyalty.

Otherwise there is little difference between the groups except by length of stay in Rhodesia. Again it is notable that the oldest established group stayed longer and left later than others.

Year of leaving	<70	71-74	75-79	80-83	84-89	90-95
Years in Rhodesia	21	22	27	31	34	35

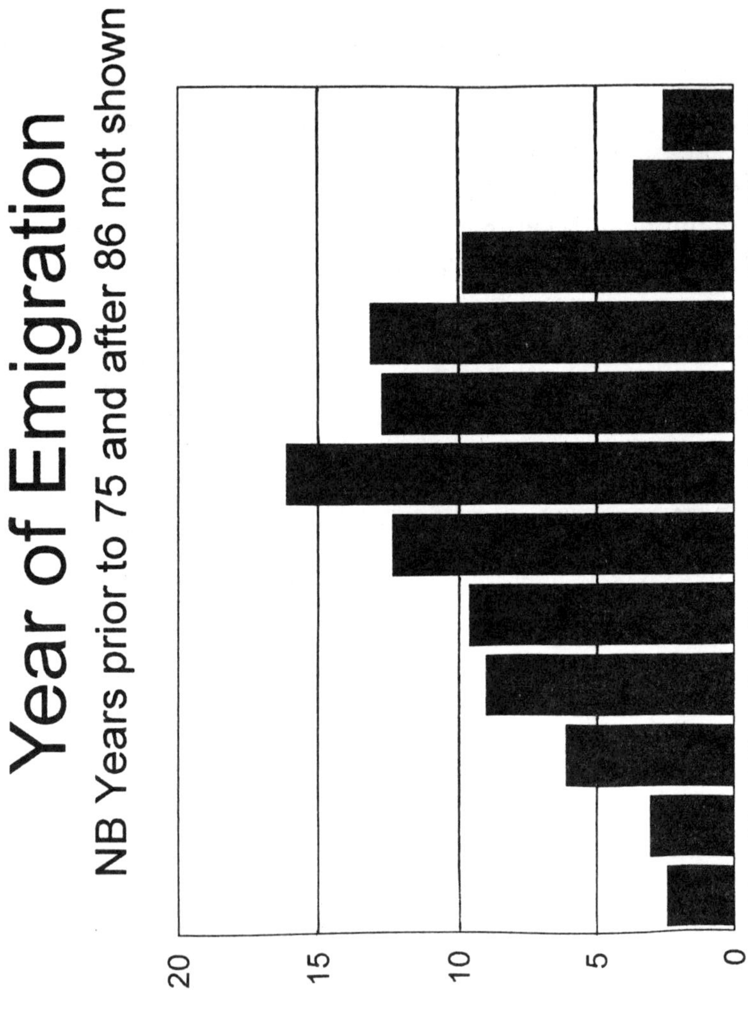

Year of Emigration
NB Years prior to 75 and after 86 not shown
0
5
10
15
20
75
76
77
78
79
80
81
82
83
84
85
86

Decade of leaving

Sixties	4%
Seventies	28
Eighties	64
Nineties	3

Again there are marked differences in the decade groups. Although South Africa and the United Kingdom have always been the major destinations for Rhodesians there was more migration to the USA in the sixties and seventies. New Zealand became more popular in the nineties. The United Kingdom was most popular in the seventies and the nineties. Australia maintained a consistent average through all the decades.

In a similar way the sixties were the times when those with less than 20 years residence left, the seventies were the period when those with under 30 years residence left and those with over 30 years residence left in the eighties and nineties. This partially reflects a greater dedication among those with long residence and, possibly, waiting until pensions became due.

Times returned to Rhodesia/Zimbabwe

To visit friends/family	3.7
Business	3.0
Holiday	2.9

Many made combined visits which made exact calculation difficult. South Africans, due to their proximity, had made more visits than any other country. Australians had made the least. This may be partially explained by the high costs of airfares between the two countries.

Education Patterns

Highest level of Education Received

	In Rhodesia	Since Rhodesia
All education before arrival	27%	-
Secondary/High	27	2
Technical qualification	16	8
University/professional	24	16
No more education	-	33

Almost a quarter of the sample had a university degree or professional qualification before arriving in Rhodesia and 16% have gained a similar qualification since leaving. Although some of this question seems to have been misunderstood, judging by personal analysis of the questionnaires it indicates a high level of appreciation of the value of education. This level is substantially lower among South African residents but can be explained to a large extent by the older age profile of those Rhodesians who emigrated to South Africa. The highest levels of education, post Rhodesia are in the USA and New Zealand - both of which have relatively young age profiles. Overall young Rhodesians seem a well-educated group (see Table below). By any definition having 43% of a population with professional or university qualifications is a remarkable achievement, especially when a substantial proportion would not benefit from receiving "local" fees - which are usually lower than those charged outsiders.

University/Professional Qualifications gained since leaving Rhodesia

By Country of Residence

Total	SA	UK	Aus	NZ	Canada	USA	Other
16%	8	20	18	33	20	39	19

By Age Group

<40	41-50	51-60	61-70	71-90
43%	27	15	3	3

Two countries - New Zealand and the USA stand out for their high levels of qualifications.

Employment Patterns

Current Employment

Same job type in same industry as Rhodesia	16%
Same job type in different industry	10
Different job type in similar industry	7
Different job type in different industry	23
(Retired/student/other)	15

The highest proportions of those who remained in the same job type in the same industry live in "other" countries. These are mainly a small group of professional security force or technical personnel such as aviation. The Canadian group are most likely to stick to the same job type but in a different industry while the Australians and New Zealanders are more likely to have different jobs but within similar industries. The Americans have made the biggest leap with almost half (45%) changing both job and industry. Born Rhodesians are more likely to have stayed in the same job and industry. The degree of movement is also related to age and education - older people and the professionally educated stay closer to the jobs and industries they knew in Rhodesia.

Time taken to find employment

Average period	2.5 months

The shortest period (1.7 months) was in New Zealand and other countries. In South Africa the period was non significantly higher at 1.8 months. This may be because many

South African settlers often managed to arrange jobs in South Africa from Rhodesia before leaving. The longest period was 3.1 months in the United Kingdom and the USA. In the case of the USA difficulties stemmed as much from bureaucratic difficulties with residence and work permits as with the economic situation. The unemployment period was longer for those who left after 1984 but this probably reflects the economic situation in the host countries. Females took a month longer than males to find work but this was often due to them staying home to set up the new household while the husband went out to work.

Number of times job changed.

The average respondent has changed jobs 2.9 times. South African residents are more static with only 2.1 job changes (possibly also due to the higher number of retired people) and US residents have changed most (3.8). Overall changes have been more common in the younger group. As would be expected the longer the period since leaving Rhodesia the more a person has changed jobs. Females have also changed jobs more often than males.

Last Employment in Rhodesia

Business - employed	25%
Government	24
Professional services	12
Technical - employed	8
Regular in Security Forces	7
Business - self employed	7
Student	5

Migration patterns vary dramatically according to employment in Rhodesia. Almost a quarter of the sample was civil servants or other government employees. Almost three quarters of these groups went to South Africa or the United Kingdom. Almost half the group of Security Force regulars had spent 21-30 years in Rhodesia and left in 1980-83. Presumably many of this group were recruited for the Federal Forces and remained until pensions were due. A further 7% was self employed businessmen who headed mainly for New Zealand or Canada but gave the United Kingdom a wide berth. Two thirds of the pensioners emigrated to South Africa. A high proportion of the professional service staff went to the United Kingdom and USA. A substantial number of self-employed professional service people went to "other" countries - outside the mainstream of settlement.

Employment Comparison

	In Rhodesia	Now
Government	24%	5
Security Forces	7	1
Self employed business	7	10
Business - employed	25	17
Professional service self employed	3	5
Professional service employed	12	13
Technical	8	6
Unemployed	-	2
Pensioner paid from Rhodesia	3	13
Pensioner paid from outside Rhodesia	-	8
Pensioner from several sources	-	7
Student	5	-

Over a quarter of the sample (28%) is now retired but only about half (13%) of that group rely on a pension from Zimbabwe. The growth in self employment is also substantial but probably in line with the general trend in western economies. Some 18% are in the professional category which is high and the proportion is even higher among the born Rhodesians. Self employment is considerably higher among born Rhodesians in the business and technical spheres than for others but not so in the professional sphere where employment by others is higher. This is highest in the USA but lowest in the United Kingdom - which has the highest unemployment rate.

Pensioners paid exclusively from Zimbabwe are most likely to reside in South Africa and have the least education, but those with pensions from other or multiple sources are more likely to live in the United Kingdom. Many of these were born in the United Kingdom and may have some pension benefits dating from before their emigration to Rhodesia or may benefit from the social security system in the United Kingdom. The highest proportion of government servants is in Australia (9%)

Demographics

Gender

Almost three quarters (74%) of the respondents were male. This is partially because the instruction specified the questionnaire should be completed by the head of the household. These proportions are higher in South Africa and the USA but lower in the United Kingdom. Women are more highly represented in the younger (under 40) age group, the over 71 age group and the lesser educated group, while men are more represented in the intermediate 41-60 age groups.

Age

The mean age of respondents is 57 years with South Africa being the oldest country at almost 61 and the USA being the youngest at under 49 years. The "oldest" organization is the Rhodesia Christian Group and the youngest is the USA organization. There were several respondents aged 90 or more - a very gratifying response.

Marital situation

Single	6%
Rhodesian married to Rhodesian	38
Rhodesian married to non Rhodesian	23
Widowed/divorced	20
Other	12

The United Kingdom has the highest proportion of the young and single. These appear to be mainly the children of UK settlers. The Rhodesians married to Rhodesians are most common in South Africa, Australia and Canada. The Rhodesians who have married non Rhodesian partners are most common in New Zealand and the USA. The widowed and divorced, together with the others (where many of the elderly placed themselves) are strongest in South Africa and the United Kingdom. Interestingly there is a higher degree of marriage among those with professional qualifications. Technically trained people are more common among "others" and other educational levels among the widowed/divorced.

Marital Status Changes

Same marital status as Rhodesia	65%
Single but married since Rhodesia	11
Widowed from Rhodesian spouse	10
Divorced/separated from Rhodesian spouse	4
Single, married and divorced since Rhodesia	3
Divorced/separated/remarried	3
Widowed from Rhodesian spouse but remarried	2

It is interesting that almost two thirds of Rhodesians have remained with the same spouses since their Rhodesian days, given the high divorce rate that occurred in Rhodesia. This group predominates in the 50-70 year age group and those who left Rhodesia during the 80's. As a sideline the most devoted group appears to be the members of the BSAP Association, 82% of who are still with the same spouse and, to a lesser extent, members of Rhodesians Worldwide.

The widowed group is strongly female, South African born and resident and with an unspecified education. If this group is added to those still with the same spouse then almost three quarters of the respondents would have been with their original spouses.

The group that married since leaving Rhodesia is predominantly the young (under 50), Rhodesian born, who left Rhodesia prior to 1975, with a professional training, ambivalent feelings about UDI and those resident in the USA. The same group (except the professionals) is also strongly represented in the "single, married and divorced since Rhodesia".

Those who have divorced their Rhodesian spouse are most common among United Kingdom and USA residents, are in their 40's, and who left Rhodesia prior to 1970 after spending under 20 years there i.e., mainly as children. This group also has ambivalent feelings about UDI and tends not to belong a Rhodesian association.

The divorced but remarried group has many similar characteristics to the divorced except they tend to be a decade older.

Greater difficulty in settling in new country

Husband	11%
Wife	14
Both same	20
N/A.	55

(Only asked of couple who were both Rhodesians). Husbands in their 50's had more trouble in settling than any other age group and this also increased with the length of time spent in Rhodesia. South African residents were more likely to consider both spouses had equal difficulties.

Nationality Changes

	At birth	Rho-desia	Now
Joint Rhodesian/other	10%	25	2
Rhodesian/Zimbabwean	22	29	3
South African	13	6	18
United Kingdom	45	20	47
Australian	-	-	10
Canadian	-	-	3
USA	-	-	3
Other Europe	3	1	4
Other country	1	-	2

While most obviously held passports of the country they were born in at birth 36% of South African born Rhodesians held Rhodesian/Zimbabwean nationality only compared to 29% overall. Possibly this indicates the wider acceptance of Rhodesian passports before UDI when compared to South African ones. Supporters of UDI were more likely have only Rhodesian passports but it is unclear whether this is cause or effect. Professionally trained people were more likely to be joint Rhodesian/other holders while technically trained ones were more likely to be United Kingdom holders.

Most Rhodesians have now adopted (or re-adopted) the passports of the country where they reside but it is noteworthy that Rhodesians, born outside the United Kingdom are less likely to take United Kingdom passports. It is unclear whether this is due to living in other countries or difficulties in getting a British passport. In a similar way, adoption of a "local" passport increases with time since leaving Rhodesia - i.e., as people spend longer in their new country they become eligible for a passport (and possibly desire to identify with the new home).

Current South African passport holders are more likely to consider UDI a success and those with only a Rhodesian/ Zimbabwean passport consider it a failure.

Current residence

Own house	58%
Own apartment/condo/townhouse	10
Rent house	11
Rent apartment	11
Stay with friends/relatives	3
Other (room, tied housing, shelter, home)	7

Over two thirds have managed to purchase either a house or apartment/flat. House ownership is highest in Australia and New Zealand and lowest in the United Kingdom and "other" countries, among born Rhodesians, males and professionally trained people. It also increases directly in line with time since leaving Rhodesia. This also agrees with the declining number of people staying with relatives as the time since leaving Rhodesia increases. The median point is about 10 years - by this time about half of those who have houses have already bought them. House ownership is strongest in the 40-60 age group. It is much weaker among the over 70 age group - who are much more likely to own apartments. Rental of houses declines directly in line with time since departure from Rhodesia

Ownership of flats/apartments and condos is stronger among those in South Africa, aged over 61 and female. The over 70 age group (especially females) is much more likely to live with relatives or friends or in "other" accommodation - often sheltered housing or senior citizen complexes. Those who considered UDI a failure are more likely to own houses or apartments than those who considered it a success.

Membership of Rhodesian Associations

The results of this question are somewhat biased as the main form of distribution of the questionnaire was through these organizations. However some 16% of questionnaires were returned by people who were not members of any organization. Often they had received photocopies from organization members.

Rhodesians Worldwide	59%
RASA/Flame Lily Foundation	26
BSAP Association	5
Rhodesian Army Association	4
RAWA	4
Rhodesia Christian Group	3
Rhodesian Association USA	3
Rhodesian Air Force Association	3
RW Ontario	2
RW New Zealand	1

Numbers add to over 100% as categories are not mutually exclusive and many members belonged to a territorial group and an ex-service group. However two groups account for the great majority of membership - South Africa and Rhodesians Worldwide. The latter as the "senior" organization has a world wide membership, while the other territorial ones are confined to that specific territory for practical purposes.

Association membership reflects the territorial distribution with the youngest members being in the USA, the middle aged in the United Kingdom and the oldest in South Africa.

Over three quarters of the BSAP membership is in the United Kingdom or South Africa, with the latter predominating. The Air Force and Army Associations have a converse distribution - more in the United Kingdom than South Africa. The Army Association is surprisingly strong in New Zealand. There is also a strong cross membership between the BSAP and the Army Association.

The Rhodesia Christian Group has a very highly skewed age profile - almost two thirds of the membership are over 60 and almost half live in South Africa. "Non" members of associations are more common among the younger age groups as must be expected.

Attitudes and Opinions

Agreement with Opinion Statements

NB. This 5 point scale is graded from 1= strongly agree to 5 = strongly disagree. 3 is the mid point (not sure).

Statement	Mean
I would return to live in Zimbabwe if possible	3.4
I would return to Zimbabwe for a holiday	1.8
My economic situation is better now than in Rhodesia	2.7
Overall I regret leaving Rhodesia	3.3
I believe my future is secure here	2.4
Overall UDI was a success	2.9
Most Zimbabweans are poorer than they were in Rhodesia	2.0
I'm still proud to be called a Rhodesian	1.5
I try to forget Rhodesia and think about the future	3.4
I try to socialize with Rhodesians	2.2
Overall Zimbabwe has done better than I expected	3.1

The table above summarizes all scores into means. This is useful but may conceal statistical anomalies which can be revealed by the chart below - where the distribution of the scores is visible.

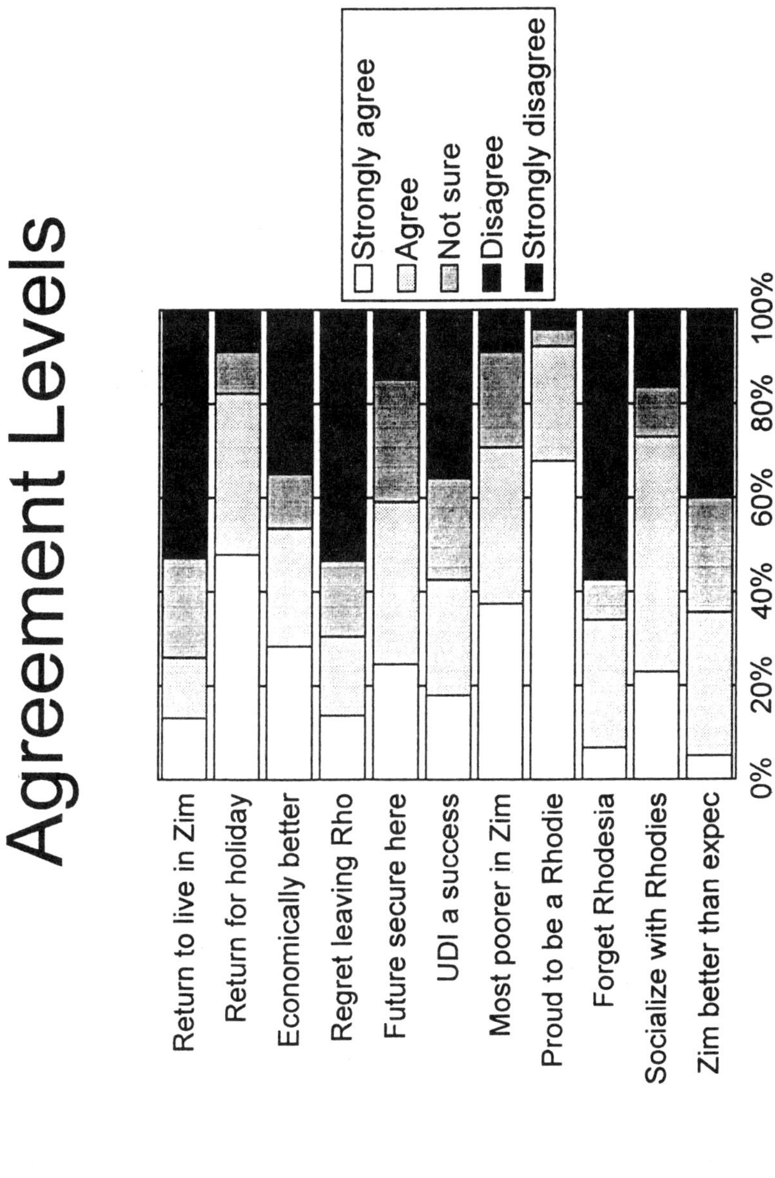
Agreement Levels
Strongly agree
Agree
Not sure
Disagree
Strongly disagree
Return to live in Zim
Return for holiday
Economically better
Regret leaving Rho
Future secure here
UDI a success
Most poorer in Zim
Proud to be a Rhodie
Forget Rhodesia
Socialize with Rhodies
Zim better than expec
0%
20%
40%
60%
80%
100%

Inclination to return to live in Zimbabwe declines with age and length of residence in Rhodesia i.e., the younger people are keener to return to live although the strongest opinion only rates a 3.0 (undecided). Also the longer people have been away the less they desire to return - probably indicating acclimatization to their new environment. However its noteworthy that almost a quarter of the respondents would certainly consider returning to live in Zimbabwe. This statement correlates highly with "Overall Zimbabwe has done better than I expected" (see below for details).

Desire to return for a holiday is similarly linked to age but remains much stronger across all age groups. Almost three quarters of the sample would return for a holiday.

Most believe that they are now better off than in their Rhodesian days with a mean score of 2.7. However there are interesting differences. US residents agree more strongly with the statement than any other country but United Kingdom residents disagree and agreement declines with age. Agreement also rises according to the length of time since respondents left Rhodesia. Overall it appears that only the very old group disagrees - presumably due to pension and economic problems and that most Rhodesians who had age on their side have overcome their losses resulting from emigration.

Most do not regret leaving Rhodesia with a mean score of 3.3. Those who regret it most left Rhodesia most recently (since 1990 - and presumably have not yet integrated themselves full into their new environments.) Regret at leaving declines with number of years spent there. Interestingly there is more agreement with this statement among those who believed UDI to be a success and the Rhodesian Christian Group than others.

Most believe their future to be secure in their current country, with the sole exception (sic) of South African residents who are undecided. The most secure country is Australia, followed by New Zealand, Canada, the USA and then the United Kingdom, although the differences are not significant.

There is slight overall agreement (2.9) with "Overall UDI was a success" with the highest agreement being among South African residents and the lowest among US residents. The highest level of agreement was among those who left in the 71-74 period but those who left in the 75-79 period are much less likely to agree. This period coincides with the general realization starting about 1975 that the war was unwinnable. UDI was also felt to be much more of a success among the technically educated rather than among the professionals. The group that felt it to be a real success was the Rhodesia Christian Group. while the non members of any group were much less convinced.

There is a much stronger level of agreement that most Zimbabweans are poorer than in the days of Rhodesia. This feeling is much stronger among those who left from 1984 onwards when the heavy inflation rate started to take a major toll of living standards among and also among the Rhodesia Christian Group. It is lower among those who felt UDI to be a failure.

The strongest agreement of all the statements was "I am still proud to be called a Rhodesian" with a mean score of 1.5. This is strongest in Canada, but weakest in the USA (although it is still strong). It also increases with the length of time spent in Rhodesia. It is weakest among those who considered UDI a failure and those who belong to no Rhodesian organization. Nevertheless it still remains the strongest level of agreement with 89% of the sample agreeing and indicates an extremely high level of pride in being Rhodesian.

There is substantial disagreement with the "I try to forget Rhodesia and think about the future". It is weakest among opponents of UDI and those who have spent less time in Rhodesia.

"I try to socialize with Rhodesians" scores highly (2.2 mean) and increases with time spent in Rhodesia. It is lowest among those who considered UDI a failure and those who belong to no Rhodesian Association (sic).

"Overall Zimbabwe has done better than I expected" rates slight disagreement at 3.1 but this is more marked in South African residents and decreases with age and time spent in Rhodesia.

These statements were subjected to a correlation analysis to find levels of agreement. This is a statistical technique which shows that increasing agreement with one statement also means increasing agreement with another. All the statements were correlated with each other thus giving a triangular shaped matrix. Due to space limitations this has been stretched over two pages.

If a minus sign is shown before a sign it means inverse correlation (increasing agreement with one statement means decreasing agreement with another.) Each group of 3 sets of figures below shows the following. The value (between -1 and +1) shows the correlation coefficient. 1 means perfect correlation. Minus 1 means perfect inverse correlation. Values close to zero mean no correlation.

The second figure is the number of people who answered that statement (less than 1460 in all cases). The third figure is the significance level. As usual only pay attention to it if it is less than 0.05. Please note that a high correlation does not imply that agreement on one statement *caused* agreement on the other.

As an example there is a high level of agreement between the statements about returning to live and returning for a visit, indicating that the persons who agreed with one statement tended to agree with the other. The coefficient of .4866 is high. There were 1289 respondents who answered both questions and the significance level is extremely high (0.0001 - indicating a possible chance of error of less than one in ten thousand.

	Return to live	Return for visit	Economic Situation	Regret leaving	Secure Future
Return for visit	.4866 1289 .0001				
Economic situation is better than Rhodesia	-.1042 1286 .0004	.0732 1328 .0076			
Overall I regret leaving	.5488 1273 .0001	.2530 1309 .0001	-.1466 1303 .0001		
I believe my future is secure here	-.2443 1284 .0001	-.0286 1333 .2962	.2988 1331 .0001	-.2153 1316 .0001	
Overall UDI was a success	.0904 1281 .0016	-.0238 1328 .6095	-.0535 1327 .0482	.1635 1307 .0001	-.0898 1339 .0014
Most Zimbabweans are poorer than in Rhodesia	.0057 1284 .8318	-.0702 1331 .0101	-.0864 1328 .0020	.0559 1315 .0401	-.0387 1346 .1522
I am still proud to be called a Rhodesian	.1403 1299 .0001	.0786 1343 .0042	-.0891 1338 .0015	.1719 1324 .0001	-.0657 1358 .0147
I try to forget Rhodesia and concentrate on the future	-.2280 1261 .0001	-.1275 1304 .0001	.0608 1310 .0260	-.2040 1288 .0001	.0987 1316 .0006
Try to socialize with Rhodesians	.1788 1278 .0001	.0979 1323 .0007	-.0975 1320 .0007	.1988 1301 .0001	-.0747 1335 .0064
Overall Zimbabwe has done better then expected	.2965 1291 .0001	.2732 1340 .0001	.0243 1336 .6217	.1511 1318 .0001	.0568 1354 .0344

	UDI was success	Zimbabweans are poorer	Proud to be Rhodie	Forget Rhodesia	Try to Socialize
Most Zimbab- weans are poorer	.1548 1346 .0001				
Still proud to be called a Rhodesian	.2836 1354 .0001	.1357 1361 .0001			
Forget Rhodesia and concentrate	-.1651 1313 .0001	-.0788 1317 .0045	-.2931 1328 .0001		
Try to socialize with Rhodies	.2155 1330 .0001	.0979 1334 .0006	.3066 1354 .0001	-.2852 1314 .0001	
Zimbabwe done better than expected	.0878 1346 .0017	-.1314 1356 .0001	-.0650 1366 .0155	-.0044 1326 .8665	.0108 1347 .6946

The highest level of agreement is between "Overall I regret leaving Rhodesia" and "I would return to live" at .5488. The second highest agreement is mentioned above "Return to live/ return for a visit." at .4866. This is followed by "Proud to be a Rhodesian/ socialize with Rhodesians" at .3066. This is closely followed by "Overall Zimbabwe has done better than expected/ Return to live" at .2965

Main Reason for leaving Rhodesia/Zimbabwe

This question was recorded in open ended, text format. The program used (The Survey System) can record and convert key words and phrases to numeric values. Many of the key words in the section were suggested by Professor Cheater. Multiple mentions within each group are possible, so results may add to more than 100%.

Rejection of majority rule	27%
Family/marriage reasons	19
Future/stability	17
Education	17
Employment	14
Economic/Financial	7
Concern for standards	6
War	5
Retirement	3
Travel/forex	2
Medical	1

In this question the answers have been grouped into categories of words with similar meanings. The category of "Rejection of maj ority rule" includes the following words:

Politic	Govern	Black	Communis
Zimbabwe	Independ	Majorit	

The key words are truncated to allow the program to match related ideas. For example "politic" includes: politics, political, politician. It is interesting the different word emphases within each of these groups that reflect both a difference in language and approach in many cases.

In the first category of "rejection of majority rule" the words "politic" and "independ" are more common among United Kingdom residents, while "govern(ment),(ing)" are more common among residents of South Africa and Australia. "Black" and "majorit" are more common among those who left in 75-79 and "govern" and "communis" among those who left in 80-83, reflecting the different themes that motivated each group. Overall residents of the USA were less worried by majority rule than any other group.

Family reasons revolved mainly round "wido" and "famil". Both of these reasons were strongest among South African residents, females and the over 71 age group. This indicates that many of this group left Rhodesia on or after being widowed to join their children, resident in other countries. As more Rhodesians settled in South Africa than any other country this motive was more prevalent among South African residents.

Future and stability were strong motivating factors, especially among males and those who settled in Australia, 28% of whom mentioned "stability" compared to an overall 14%. Related words of "instability" and "secur" were also more common among this group. Significantly mentions of "future" and "uncertain" were weaker among those settling in South Africa.

Education ranked equally with stability as a reason for leaving. However it was particularly high among those heading for South Africa and low among those going to the USA. Partially this reflects the age distribution - the problem was most worrisome to the 41-60 age groups. Twenty years ago this group would have children at primary school or about to attend one. Educational integration was a major objective of the new government and one that would immediately affect them. This feeling was weaker among those who left in 75-79 (before substantial integration occurred) but much stronger among those who left in 80-83 when it had just been applied and most had personal experience of the situation. It was also stronger among males and those with a professional training.

Employment was a major factor for leaving at 14%. In comparison to education above where one single word "educat" comp rised nearly 15% of the 17% mention, the employment related mentions were much more diverse.

Employ	4%
Job	3
Contract	3
Transfer	2
Career	2

Younger emigrants (under 40) were more likely to be seeking careers, while the older groups were seeking "employ" or "jobs" - a subtle difference. Those born in South Africa or the United Kingdom, who had spent under 10 years in Rhodesia and left before 1974 were more likely to reach the end of a contract. This obviously reflects the decline in recruitment of contract workers in the post UDI period.

"Transfer", "career" and "job" also featured more strongly among the professionally trained group.

Economic and financial reasons are obviously linked to employment. Both reasons particularly motivated United Kingdom residents to leave. It was also a major factor among those leaving between 1984-89 when several years of socialist policies by the government were starting to show their results. Worries about business conditions were stronger among those who left in 71-74 but overall economic conditions were a minor motivating factor for those leaving between 75-79.

The concern for (declining) "standard" and "servic" were most common among South African residents, and among those born in "other" countries. Many of these had been born in other African territories and had presumably witnessed the problems experienced after independence in these countries. Many of these also formed part of the 80-83 exodus, again presumably having experienced the sharp deterioration in standards that occurred with the rapid Africanisation of most government posts.

Surprisingly "war" accounted for only 5% of decisions to leave and was concentrated very largely among those who left between 1971- 79 (sic), those who went to Canada and those who believed UDI to be a failure.

Retirement was obviously concentrated among the older group and among those who left in the 84-89 period, presumably when pensions became due.

Travel was almost equally ranked with retirement but was almost the converse being concentrated among the young and those who were born in Rhodesia.

Main Reason for Second Move

Employment	7%
Family/marriage	6
South Africa	5
Economic/financial	4
Politics	2
Socio cultural	2
Weather	2
Future stability	2
Retirement	1

Only 20% of the respondent answered this question so the base is 300 rather than 1460. Nevertheless distinct patterns emerge.

Employment related problems were the major motivator in all countries, except South Africa. They were also stronger among the professionally trained.

The family/marriage includes a high proportion of widows(ers) joining their children in other countries.

Although the South Africa mention was predominantly from those who left the country, approximately 20% of this group had immigrated to South Africa from other countries, after leaving Rhodesia. Females disliked South Africa more than males.

Among those who mentioned economics and financial problems money was the major mention from former United Kingdom residents.

Most of those who mentioned politics or socio cultural reasons for leaving are professionally trained who left South Africa.

Future stability was also a concern from former South African residents. Most of these went to the United Kingdom on their second move. Dislike of the climate was almost exclusively a British phenomenon.

Main Thing missed about Rhodesia/Zimbabwe

Lifestyle	40%
Friendship	36
Country	28
People	25
Climate	24
Africa	7
Pride/patriotism	5

Obviously most Rhodesians highly appreciated the lifestyle of their land. South African residents miss it most and New Zealand residents least. US residents obviously feel the more hurried pace of life in their new country.

South African residents strongly miss friends and the spirit of camaraderie but United Kingdom residents do not feel this loss so strongly. The converse is true about the countryside - United Kingdom residents miss the bush and especially the space more than South African residents do. The lack of wild life is a loss to Australasians.

South Africans also miss the people much more than other groups, although the Canadians and New Zealanders also miss family and relatives.

Climatic mentions are very country specific, as may be imagined. The United Kingdom, Canada and New Zealand groups strongly dislike their climate, the Australians and South Africans do not have this problem and the US residents are in the middle. The born Rhodesians worry less about climates than those born in the United Kingdom.

The feeling for Africa still remains strong among all groups except the British and the South Africans miss the honesty, the efficiency and tolerance of Rhodesia. Again the British miss these aspects less than any other group.

Under the heading of pride the Rhodesian born and South African residents miss honesty and efficiency more than any other country.

Conscious retention of Rhodesian Life and Culture

Friends	18%
None	7
Standards	6
Outdoor	5
Hospitality	5
Honesty	5
Contacts	4

Retention of old friends and friendships is the most important factor, especially among the South African residents, those who believed UDI a success and the over 60 age group.

The second most popular answer of "none" or "nothing" comes from the youngest age group, who spent less than 10 years in Rhodesia, who believed UDI to be a failure and belong to no organization - the converse.

The decline in standards was noted most by Australian residents. The retention of honesty was very strong in South Africa but weak in the United Kingdom. Retention of "all" or "everything" was very strong among South African residents and the over 70 group.

Major Problems in First Country of Settlement

Cultural aspects	30%
Financial	19
Employment	16
Homesick for family	11
Accommodation	11
None	10
Language	9
Lack of familiar items	8
Attitudes of locals	8
Climate	7
Own attitudes	3
Education	2
Bureaucracy/Administrative	2

The Canadians suffered most from cultural aspects with a 49% score compared to an overall 30%. The financial constraints were felt most by Australians, those who left between 75-79 and the 41-50 age group (who would probably have young children at that time). The oldest group (71-99 years) suffered least from financial restraints - possibly because they had pensions to draw on which were more freely transferable, although capital assets usually remained frozen in Rhodesia. The professionally educated experienced more cultural shock than the technically educated who noted a change in life style more, although this may be a difference in terminology.

UK settlers suffered most with employment, followed by Australia. South African settlers suffered least in this regard - probably because of the much closer links between the two countries and the proximity which enabled job seeking visits to be made much more easily. The job environment in South Africa was also more similar to that in Rhodesia, thus easing the transition.

Homesickness was the third problem and affected New Zealand residents and females to far greater extent than others.

Accommodation was a problem of similar magnitude to homesickness but was felt more keenly by United Kingdom residents and the oldest groups.

A tenth of the sample experienced no problems in settling but this figure was almost double in New Zealand and also higher among females (despite their problems with homesickness above)

Language problems were experienced mainly by South African residents, especially those who had spent most of their lives in Rhodesia, although those who settled in non-English speaking countries also suffered.

Eight percent noticed the lack of certain items. Given that Rhodesia was very short of many goods due to sanctions and this probably relates to lack of certain familiar brands and foodstuffs.

A similar percentage had problems with local attitudes. The only major deviation was among the group who believed UDI to be a success who had more problems - which may indicate a lack of adaptability on their own part.

Nearly 7% complained of the climate. This was particularly strong in the United Kingdom and to a lesser extent in Canada and the USA. It was also noticeable among those who believed UDI a success and, strangely, among those who had spent least time in Rhodesia. This problem declined in line with time since departure indicating some acceptance over time.

Only 3% believed their own attitudes, mainly a sense of loss, created a problem but this was much stronger in New Zealand and slightly stronger among females.

Education was not a major problem overall but among those with young children, US residents (wild and feral children was one description) and professionally trained people it was much more of a problem.

Pension problems were experienced by under 1% but in Australia this level was double. Driving was a problem to a few - mainly the elderly and females.

Interestingly 22% did not answer this question. If we add the 9% who claimed to experience no problems then nearly a third seem to have had no problems worth noting.

Major Problems in current country

Financial	28%
Politics	21
Cultural aspects	12
Business	9
Crime/security	7
(lack of) Friends	5
Exchange control	5
None	7

Over a quarter of the respondents suffered financial problems but this was much more marked in two countries - the United Kingdom and South Africa and among the older respondents.

In the United Kingdom the problems were generally related to finance but in South Africa pension and related problems (cost of living, inflation) problems were more noticeable. This is also linked to devaluation of the Z$ and general forex restrictions suffered by a higher proportion of South African residents than any other country. The "other" educational group suffered financial problems while members of the BSAP Association and the Rhodesia Christian

Group suffered more financial problems than other associations.

Overall it appears that those currently aged under 50 (and thus probably in their twenties or thirties at the time of emigration) suffered least and have managed to re-establish themselves financially.

Just over a fifth experienced political problems but, again this was almost a third in South Africa but under 16% in the United Kingdom. Education was a larger problem for those in the USA - again the younger profile, indicating the greater likelihood of young children and the well-deserved reputation for mediocrity in American schools plays a part.

Cultural problems were particularly marked among the younger (and more Rhodesian born) and those who lived outside the mainstream of settlement in non English speaking and alien environments such as the Middle and Far East.

Business and career problems affected the younger and, to a lesser extent those in the United Kingdom and Australia.

Crime and security were major problems in South Africa and (non significantly) in the USA. This was much less of a problem in the United Kingdom and, especially Australia. Corruption was also seen as a problem in South Africa.

The country with least current problems appears to be Canada and the "other" countries.

Housing is more of a problem in South Africa than any other country. Lack of friends is a peculiarly Australian problem - especially with a feeling of isolation and distance. This may be linked to the lower number of return visits to Zimbabwe by Australians than any other country. This is probably due to the high airfares and infrequent flights between Australia and southern Africa.

Although attitudes were not a serious problem with under 2% mentioning them it mainly occurred in the United Kingdom.

This table was subjected to a statistical technique called correspondence analysis which links attributes (problems) with countries. It is also called perceptual mapping. Where problems and countries are physically close together on the map they are perceived as being associated. The United Kingdom and Canada are seen as similar (close together) and suffer problems of: climate, finance and life-style. Australia suffers from (lack of) friends and South Africa is closely associated with crime, uncertain future, politics, affirmative action and language. Housing and currency devaluation problems are problems in several countries (New Zealand, USA, South Africa) but less so in Australia (which has the highest level of home owners) and seems to have a more generous attitude towards pensions.

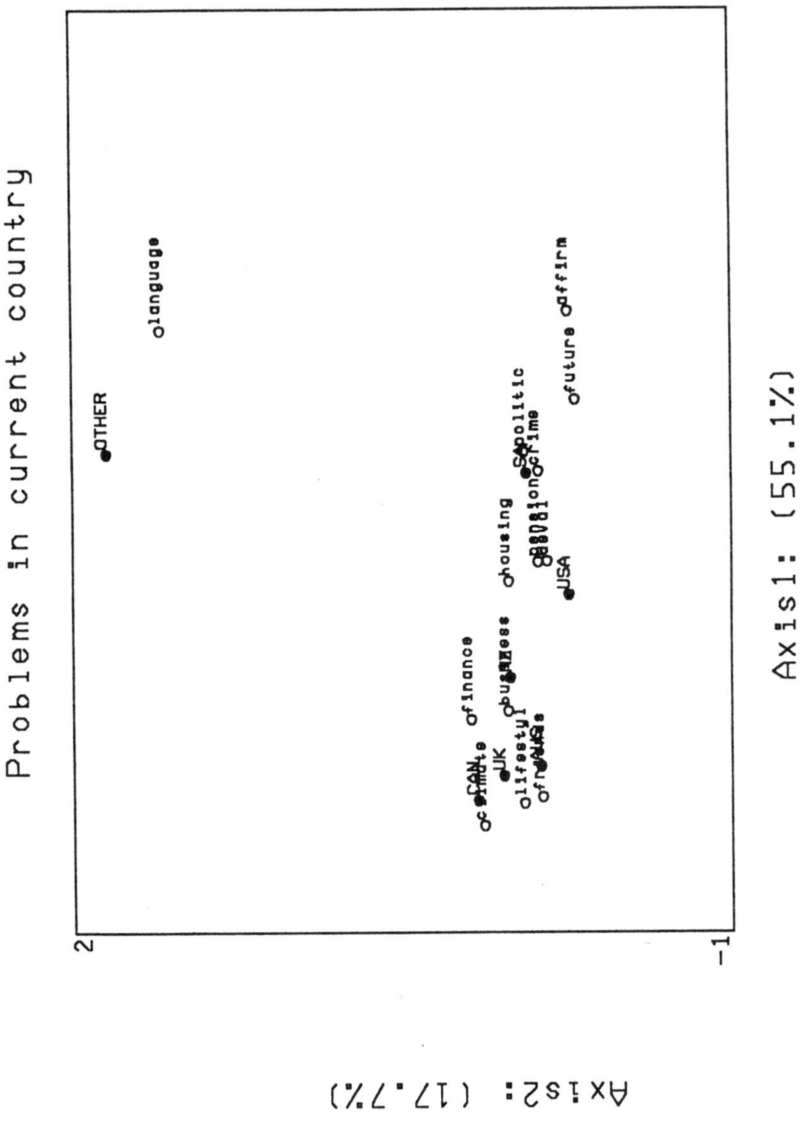
Problems in current country
OTHER
language
future
affirm
politic
crime
housing
USA
finance
UK
CAN
lifestyl
2
-1
Axis1: (55.1%)
Axis2: (17.7%)

Most Liked Aspects of current country

Space/environment/nature	16%
Stability/opportunity	11
Local people, history, culture	11
Health, education, travel, housing	10
Politics	10
Choice/variety of goods	9
Local attitudes/behaviour	8
Consumption	7
Climate	7
Family ties	5
Nothing	4
Cultural facilities	4
Leisure	4

The beauty of the English countryside is appreciated by many respondents while Australia and New Zealand gain points for space. Environment is not a major attraction for USA residents.

Stability and opportunity are major benefits in Australia, Canada and the USA and among the younger age groups. Australia also scores highly on security and future prospects.

The local people appear friendliest in New Zealand but culture and history score high points in the United Kingdom. A further benefit of the United Kingdom is the ease of travel (one respondent reported the best part of Britain was Gatwick) and the health services. Travel and education scored lowly in South Africa. Political freedom was rated highly in Australia but low in South Africa.

The choice and variety of goods were rated very highly in the United Kingdom and the USA. This aspect received a substantial mention from those who left in the 84-89 period - a time when Zimbabwean socialist policies had reduced consumer choice almost to zero in shops.

In keeping with the friendly New Zealanders the local attitudes were highly rated, especially by the older and female respondents.

The United Kingdom climate still created problems for residents but South Africans appreciated their climate highly and the Canadians loved their spring. South Africa also rated highly for retaining family ties and kinship.

Those who liked little or nothing about their country were found mainly in the United Kingdom and were disproportionately female. However the United Kingdom's history, culture and TV programming were highly regarded, together with its proximity to Europe. New Zealand appears to have good news and library facilities.

This table was also subjected to correspondence analysis. South Africa is closely associated with the sea coast. Distance denotes non association. The United Kingdom is about as far as it can get from weather and climate thus indicating that this is not a perceived like about the country. It is, however, closely linked with culture and countryside. The USA and Canada are associated with opportunity, Australia with people and New Zealand with freedom and space.

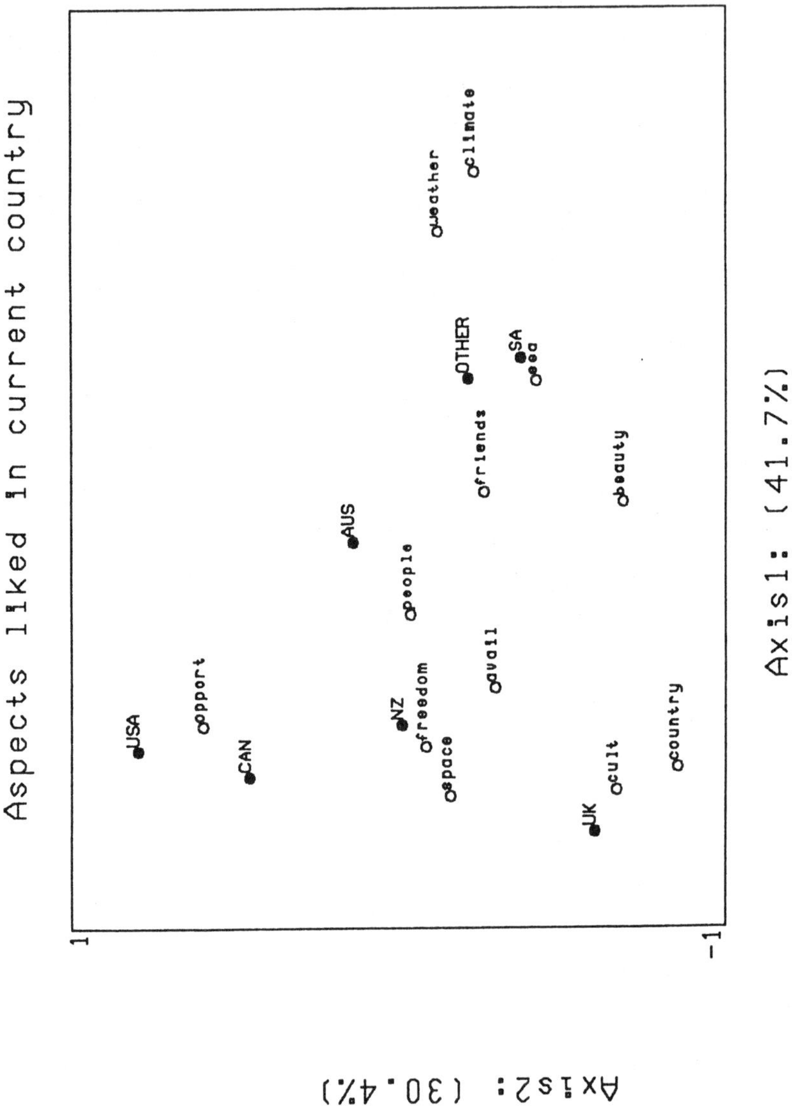
Aspects liked in current country
Axis1: (41.7%)
Axis2: (30.4%)
1
-1
USA
CAN
AUS
NZ
OTHER
SA
UK
opport
people
freedom
space
avail
weather
climate
friends
sea
beauty
cult
country

Most disliked aspect of current country

Climate	20%
Politics	17
Locals	12
Crime/instability	11
Local behaviour	9
Local attitudes	9
Bureaucracy	5
Standards/efficiency	4
Local culture/language	4
Politics of Race	4
Nothing	2

Although climate is the major individual problem it comes mainly from two countries - United Kingdom and Canada, followed by New Zealand. South Africa, Australia and the USA are significantly lower than average.

Seventeen percent dislike the politics of their new land. This is higher in South Africa and Australia and lower in the United Kingdom. Racial politics is a problem in South Africa.

The local people are narrow minded and present more of a problem in the United Kingdom than any other country, although native South Africans are considered rude and Canadians undisciplined.

Crime presents major problems to South Africans, and even more to US residents. Bureaucracy and inefficiency are substantial problems to South Africans only.

The local culture in Australia presents a problem while litter is a problem in Britain, especially among those who spent least time in Rhodesia. Isolation from family and friends presents a problem to US residents and to a lesser extent among Australians.

Who would return to Zimbabwe?

Twelve percent strongly agree and another 12% agree that they would like to return to Zimbabwe to live. Effectively almost a quarter of the sample would consider returning, even after an average 15 years away and to live under the rule of a government they formerly detested enough to leave with almost no assets. How does this group differ from the others in the sample?

This group has certain specific characteristics. They left Zimbabwe slightly later (1981 c.f. 1980) than those who would not return. They are more likely to have secondary education only or a technical qualification and have undertaken no further studies since leaving Rhodesia.

Security Force regulars and students are also keener. People employed in technical posts or unemployed are keener to return. They have made major career changes (different jobs in different industries) and it took them an average of two weeks extra to find work on arrival.

They have also changed jobs more often than average. They have returned to visit family or friends 5 times as opposed to the general 3.7 times. They have also returned more often for holidays. A high proportion lives in South Africa and has parents, siblings or children in South Africa or Zimbabwe.

They do not believe they have a secure future in their current country. There are slightly more females with an average age of 53 compared to non-returnees at 59. Widows and divorced people are more likely to want to return

A further distinguishing factor is the lack of property ownership by those who like to return - they are much more likely to rent. They are strongly represented in the BSAP Association.

The main reason for leaving Zimbabwe was for educational reasons (for their children) rather than a rejection of majority rule or lack of faith in the future. They miss the slower pace of life more than most, strongly miss the people, suffer slightly more from homesickness and strongly dislike the attitudes of the locals, their language and the climate of the country where they settled. They currently worry about employment, peace, safety, inflation and dislike the (lack of) space.

Overall they have not settled in their new country. This is particularly true in South Africa where the current turmoil has made them highly unsettled and they possibly see Zimbabwe as having overcome its teething troubles and settled down. Their extra number of return visits may well have shown an improving situation over the last few years. They may well have assets frozen in Zimbabwe that cannot be realized.

Their low ownership of fixed property partially reflects the lesser time in their new country and its unsettling effect. Often having left owner occupied houses in Rhodesia they may have a nostalgic memory of better days that time has not yet obliterated.

And that's the way it was

The following paragraphs are replies to the final question in the survey in which respondents were asked to describe major achievements, problems, strange or funny incidents since leaving Rhodesia. They cover a wide range of subjects, though several common themes emerge. Overall they give an insight into the mind of the Rhodesian that no set of numerical data can equal.

They are not presented in any order of importance or by subject - rather they are listed in the approximate order in which they were received. Only comments which relate to highly personal incidents or which disparage specific individuals were excluded.

Occasionally quotes have been shortened but this was purely because they over ran the space allocated to them by the program. Some sentences have been abbreviated for the same reasons.

In their own words

I feel it is a major achievement that a Rhodie comes to California and within 4 years is approached by a leading analytical lab to head the agronomy section when there are many others to choose from. Biggest problem is stress. There is not much time for leisure and the stress of trying to raise children in a immoral/amoral society with little decency is high. Self centeredness is a major concern. The paradox is we came to USA to give our children a better future but we still made the right decision and now are US citizens.

My grandfather arrived in Rhodesia in the late 1800's. My dad was Rhodesian born in 1908. I will always feel Rhodesia is my home. My son was born in the USA but I will ensure he has ties to Zimbabwe and our relatives there. I would return if they would permit me to work there.

My son who was 1 month old at the time is the only Rhodesian I know who was allowed into the United Kingdom with a Rhodesian passport in 1976. The South African air hostess was very intimidating when the British immigration official began questioning my son's right to enter the country.

General Walls was right when he said at Las Vegas that Rhodesia was a way of life rather than a country. I miss the way of life rather than the country. That piece of land once called Rhodesia, now Zimbabwe will be around forever but that way of life is unfortunately gone forever. I'm just glad to be to be one of the few who did experience it.

I would have remained in Rhodesia but when the government changed my life became unpleasant - phone tapped, placed under surveillance at home etc. and I was advised to leave to avoid arrest by friends in Intelligence. I was fortunate to be hired on my first day in Salisbury, first day in the United Kingdom and first day in the USA so I have not had to experience any economic hardship and personal problems because of a large network of friends. I don't think many Rhodesians were as lucky as me.

Both my wife and I have become highly respected at work due to our high standards of work ethics which is not common among the majority of US citizens employed in our area of work.

My late husband and I worked in South Africa and built 2 homes with earnings. The sale helped to supplement my husband's pension. As the years passed our pension shrank alarmingly. Today without my children's help I would be destitute. My pension is only pocket money. With the exchange rate I lost a lot of money coming to Canada but as a widow I wanted to be near my daughter and family.

Rhodesia was a good time of our lives. The rest of the world has lots to offer and we try to keep it all in perspective

Created a business and built a beautiful new home. Two children married with successful careers. Members of private golf club, wife ladies' club champion in 1990/92. When we arrived in 1980 did not have green cards (US immigration permits). It took 2 years of red tape to get it.

I am safe in Canada. Others are not so secure, pensions etc. to be considered. I am currently assisting the first coloured member of xxxx to asylum in the USA. He could tell of problems.

I have been very successful in New Zealand but always seemed to be catching up and make up for lost time. Result set up a business - put everything into it and lost everything including family from 87-92. Since then remarried, new family, good job and may have time to build asset base again before retirement.

It took coming to Canada to force me to become professionally qualified as an accountant. In Rhodesia there was not too much incentive to do that because one could get by on ability. I am able to visit Zimbabwe every 3 years and its downhill slide is disheartening after all the potential it had under white rule.

I have succeeded in the USA because I was prepared to enter the job market at entry level and let my abilities and actions speak for themselves. This resulted in my current executive position where my ability to get things done is recognized and rewarded. While I remember my days in Rhodesia with affection we are not when-wes. We are so fortunate to live in the greatest country in the world and give thanks to God for all we have. Americans are wonderful for accepting you for what you are - unlike the Poms.

I miss Rhodesia but it was a time and place that will never be again so I cherish the memories and press on with life.

Both sons settled into excellent jobs after local additional training. Both sons served in Rhodesian Army (RLI and Medical Corps) and this caused a delay in leaving Rhodesia/Zimbabwe. Both married - one to a Rhodesian lass and the other to a Canadian - now I have 4 Canadian grand daughters.

August 1938 went on holiday to see Victoria Falls. December 1938 Declared prohibited immigrant on returning to South Africa at Voortrekker time. Held in jail Mafeking 3 days. Returned to

Bulawayo Police Depot. Released and worked at Shell within 2 days. Joined army 2nd. Batt. Rhodesia Regiment at St. George's Hall Sept 4th. 1939. Transferred to RAF contingent. To England July 1940. The rest is a war story. When I write of the war it is WW2. I met a fine body of men in Rhodesia and in the Military. I will never forget them.

Despite discrimination I specialized in pathology which I love and which I could not have done in Rhodesia. Am presently Director of a lab for one of the largest community hospitals in the province. Most Rhodesians I know in Canada have done well under the circumstances. I yearn for Rhodesia but know it no longer exists and to go back to Zimbabwe would require more adjustment than moving to Canada. Zimbabwe is foreign to me. Most did not leave Rhodesia - they left Zimbabwe.

I consider I have been reasonably fortunate in establishing both myself and my family in Canada. I am now retired but am able to enjoy a fairly good standard of living. I have to give credit to the generosity of the Canadian government in the amount of social security and perquisites it provides to immigrants like myself.

I watch every documentary on central and southern Africa. My fiancée thinks I am mad to do so. I have become English in that I am to marry a local girl, my children are English and I have a totally English way of life. I miss Zimbabwe like hell for all that.

It has always interested me that most of the Rhodesians (white) I know of have done very well in their new countries. I don't think it's just our education. For some reason we pampered, privileged colonials developed a strong work ethic and our social orientation and conscience rejects the concept of social welfare assistance.

I just wish the Zimbabwe government would become more democratic, less anti-white and more economically competent then we could move back. Zimbabwe still has the nicest black people in the world, strangely enough.

It takes a lot to get used to snow and really cold weather. I know a lot left Canada because of it. It took a while for my work mates to accept that I wasn't there to take their jobs away but to contribute. I managed to open a mechanic shop part time.

After retiring from position of hospital secretary in 1979 I worked as a volunteer in the Herbarium, Salisbury. Becoming interested in mosses and liverworts I managed to publish "A Checklist of the Bryophytes of Zimbabwe" before emigrating. As a result of the publication I am privileged to work as a volunteer at the West Australian Herbarium in the same capacity. It's marvellous.

Our 2 children attended good universities in the USA which we probably would not have been able to afford if we stayed in Zimbabwe. We are frequently complimented on what "outstanding" young people we raised. Neither of our children is much different to the majority of young people they grew up with. They just have goals, work determinedly towards them and are polite, well balanced people - i.e., average Rhodesians!

UDI in hindsight was probably the biggest mistake the then current politicians made in the current history of the country. I have a very strong feeling that the path of multi-racialism discussed in the 50's and 60's would have resulted in a stronger more united country than Zimbabwe is today.

The support of other ex-Rhodesians was the greatest factor in us settling happily here. Rhodesia was a wonderful country and we privileged to live there. Our childhoods were some of the best years but it is no more.

Although I left before Rhodesia became Zimbabwe I consider myself a Zimbabwean more than a Rhodesian. I feel holding onto the old name of Rhodesia is living in the past. My experience has been that "Rhodesia" has a stigma attached to it and if I were to return to Zimbabwe it would be as the country is now, not as it was growing up. There were reasons why I left in the first place.

I have assimilated well into South African life. However I miss the camaraderie of Rhodesia and regret losing contact with most of my school friends. I am desperately keen to return on holiday and show my wife "God's own country". I would consider returning permanently should Mugabe be ousted - highly unlikely at this stage.

Attained rank of principal engineering assistant in under 10 years. This normally takes 20 or more years to attain as a contract supervisor with ESCOM

Our 4 children attended same university in Texas. We have been well received by Texans and own a home.

Both parents were Rhodesian and found it difficult to leave the country and adapt to life in the UK. Part due to age and leaving friends and seeing all they had worked for being taken from them. They passed away but I adjusted to life here. I worry that many ex-Rhodies feel UK people are unfriendly. I found the opposite and feel any unfriendliness is self induced. Rhodies keep making the same mistake of living in past and sticking together to the extent of excluding others.

Any move means a major change in lifestyle- we continue an endless search for a gardener. Our children adjusted well and are totally Australian but retain an interest in Africa from afar. If we had no friends/ relatives still in Zimbabwe we would probably put Rhodesia/Zimbabwe down to just good memories.

As a disabled war veteran I managed to get all my assets out of Zimbabwe. Zimbabwe government still pays for maintenance/ replacement of my prosthesis.

Having been retrenched when control of my employer reverted to Zimbabwe I started my own customs clearing business and have prospered in the last few years.

I took out a policy when I got married (endowment) for 25 years. It matured while I was in Canada and it bought the hall and stair carpet only. What did you sell me (insurance Co.)?

The more I learn about the US role in destroying the Rhodesian government the angrier I get and wish to emigrate to the UK.

As a Polish regular army officer before the war and taking part throughout it I could not return to my native Poland which was, by its British and American allies, ceded to Soviet Russia at Yalta. I chose to settle in Rhodesia after the war. I was happy in my work, bringing up 2 sons, making friends, backing up Ian Smith's UDI. These were 26 of the happiest years of my life but I had to leave war torn Rhodesia which incursions of communist inspired black bands, in spite of the gallant defence by the Rhodesian Army, were making the political future of this beautiful country uncertain and its' doom was eventually sealed at Lancaster House. My emigration to South Africa brought me a better position in my employment and restoration of family ties as my younger son had married and settled there. Life was very pleasant until my retirement, then seeking once more a new peaceful asylum, as South Africa became more destabilised by blacks, we landed for good, I hope, in the Isle of Man.

I loved the climate - no rain in winter - not one drop. Great for planning picnics, hiking etc. and outdoor weddings and events.

The Rhodesia we knew and loved should never have been changed.

Terrible things happened to me and my Down's (syndrome) daughter (now 24 years. old) after we left Zimbabwe. Our Christian faith sustained us and all is well now. Zimbabwe was wonderful down all those years but we would not return even for a holiday as I want no disappointment. We are thankful to be as comfortable as we are and love meeting up with other ex-Rhodies each month.

The hardest time was breaking the 3 month homesickness. Major achievement - raising 3 wonderful children. After 30 years Americans still ask if I am from Australia.

Will probably live half in Zimbabwe and half in United Kingdom in our retirement due to our circumstances.

We had a tremendous time in Rhodesia/Zambia and South Africa and have no regrets. Had we not left when we did we were in danger of being locked it due to exchange controls. Exchange rates, even today are very poor and many people cannot move if they want to. Had we not had family in the United Kingdom we would probably have moved to Australia.

Settled down fairly well apart from always feeling cold. Wife not so settled in spite of being UK born. Financially found it hard - could not have managed without help of ex-Rhodie friend and wife finding work. Self unable to work now due to age and emphysema.

We consider we were privileged to spend most of our lives in the finest country in the world. But that country is not there anymore. South Africa has been good to me. I regret Rhodesia but have no regrets about leaving Zimbabwe. After 10 years of hard work I am able to retire but have gained enough respect to have people seek me out so am only partially retired.

Set up new aerial survey company in Bloemfontein and produced first multi-coloured street maps on Bloemfontein and handled many mapping projects for both state and private institutions.

My father's "death" has never been fully explained by the authorities. His body was never found. He was one of the first to die in the Rhodesian war.

Very sorry how much money I lost in Zimbabwe due to demise of dollar. I would love to invest in Zimbabwe but am afraid of losing my investment through no fault of my own. Why does the West support Zimbabwe when they are against whites? If we did that in the United Kingdom we would be branded as racists.

Why didn't the Rhodesian government help whites who left after fighting as an officer for 10 years in regular army. We were left on our own, not even given a degree in management - boy did we manage! The top boys looked after the top boys and used us to buy them time. We were then forgotten. It's left a very bitter smear on a wonderful memory of those young men, both black and white, who died for their country.

I cannot believe that my experience of asbestos mining, sanctions breaking or the Rhodesian Army are particularly unusual ,nor any experiences since coming back to the UK.

Physically built own house, opened own business, educated children through university. Experienced employment difficulties, cultural differences, loneliness.

I am now confined to a wheelchair after bike accident but drive a car and still work. In 92 when I went to Zimbabwe I had to be carried off the plane as there are no facilities at Harare airport as at other international airports.

Found western companies buying each other and existing staff laid off. Re-employment made harder by feeble politicians lost in creating a better atmosphere for security.

I have not kept contact with old friends in Zimbabwe and regret this very much.

You Rhodesians are like the Israelites - always on the move.

In spite of the war you were safer in Rhodesia than in RSA in peace. UDI was the right thing at the right time but a settlement could have been negotiated (in hindsight) with Harold Wilson.

The people and the standards lived to will never be forgotten. Rhodesia was a political pawn and never was a threat to anyone.

Any politician should look to the total chaos in Africa to judge Rhodesia by.

Life is good in Australia. It is like living wrapped in cotton wool and fuzzy. Sometime the rest of the world will realize it is so far behind in some aspects and things will change dramatically.

Born in Chile of British parents. Served in WRNS during WW2. Met my husband who joined up from Rhodesia to serve in the Royal Navy. After marriage in 1945 my first daughter was born in United Kingdom in 46 and we were repatriated to Rhodesia where, after a years training, my husband was given a farm in 1947. We lived in Karoi growing maize and tobacco until we sold the farm in 73 and lived in Salisbury. Five years later we returned to UK. Two other daughters born in Rhodesia.

Have found a negative attitude among employers - almost racial due to having lived in South Africa. My wife also finds this among the teaching fraternity. Find people who have visited Africa much more aware of difficulties and more tolerant.

1925 arrived in Bulawayo aged 5 months. Educated at Milton and Bulawayo tech. Remember 40th. anniversary of occupation of Matabeleland. Town Hall was opened. Before it was the old market and town hall topped by a wooden tower which contained a bee hive. One Saturday morning they went wild and cleared all the whites and blacks off the streets up to the Post Office. One of the Bulawayo characters was old Mr. Williams who used to chase all the blacks with his stick. Was locked up many times in No. 1 Grey St. It was rumoured that his family was murdered in the Matabele rebellion. In 1939 the talk of Bulawayo was the nude party in the park at midnight attended by the Mayor and local dignitaries.

We chose to move to give our 2 children a better chance in life. They have both benefitted but tough for us. Our retirement (soon) looks brighter than it would be in Zimbabwe - health etc.

Left Zimbabwe reluctantly in 83 but managed with ease to obtain nursing qualifications in England. Would like to return but my husband would not get employment in ceramics field. Also feel I would not be able to adjust to the shortages and lack of choice of goods and variety and spice of life and consumables.

My major achievements are becoming a qualified nurse and mid-wife. Secondly bringing up 2 sons on my own but nowhere would it have been easier than in Rhodesia with its way of life, climate and wonderful people so caring and friendly. My sons enjoyed a happy childhood and good education. My younger son remains in Zimbabwe and still prefers it to anywhere else where the people are friendly and there is much to commend it.

I am proud to have been brought up in Rhodesia/Zimbabwe. I believe my upbringing and schooling in that nation have helped me to greatly achieve the life I have today. I am proud to be from the country whether called Rhodesia or Zimbabwe and still have good feelings for the nation despite the outward racist attitude of some of its top officials. I believe the regular people are what make the country what it is.

We see Arizona to be much like Rhodesia - weather plants, people, countryside.

I realize that the loss of our son and the subsequent death of my husband not long after we emigrated to South Africa has influenced my outlook considerably. My late husband (Rhodesian pioneer and early settler stock) used to say that we loved Rhodesia but left Zimbabwe. I am fortunate to live in a granny flat attached to my daughter's house. I thank God for that. Although I was born in the United Kingdom my father was Rhodesian - doing a mining degree there when he met and married my mother.

I worked for UCT as an administrator and took some time to accept that UCT is run by academics by loads of committees. Joined my son as a director of his business and thoroughly enjoyed the cut and thrust of business world.

Although we have adjusted and made a good life for ourselves there is still a feeling of not belonging - being on the outside looking in. We miss the close friendships and honesty of the Rhodesians. Everyone here is out to make a buck out of you.

I am 72 years old and am still working as our money left in Zimbabwe is in 4% bonds and the exchange rate is $Z 2-50 to R1.

It can be depressing having known Rhodesia because it is no longer a place to go home to. I feel very rootless and wish I could go home. Was it all worth it?

Changing countries does jeopardize plans for retirement. Emigration is expensive - will never do it again unless forced to do so.

Rhodesians have a special breed- hard working (mostly) innovative, friendly - welcoming helpful. Most of us knew we were fighting a losing battle but we kept going. I have no regrets - we had the best years of our life in that country.

The general ignorance of Rhodesia (locality, geography, history etc.) saddens us. Even blood relatives in United Kingdom expected us to be black and live in mud huts. Our sons particularly loved to wind up their teachers with "out of Africa" skits. We thank the Lord for blessing us with living and experiencing the Rhodesian heritage however short it was. Life moves on and one's attitude to it is all important.

Major problem has been sex and marital status both in UK and South Africa. A single/divorced woman with dependents is generally avoided by society - hence why I say my problem has been with people. I'm sure I would have experienced this problem wherever I went. Moving to United Kingdom was greatly assisted by the booklet published by RW "Settling in the UK". Their advice was absolutely spot on. Thank you.

My daughter settled here and is now a teacher. My son couldn't settle here and emigrated to South Africa when 20. I have settled but still feel I don't belong. My son wants to go to the USA or Australia but has no friends or relatives there. I would like to move to Devon.

Took quite a while to get children accepted as immigrants to Canada and their difficulty to find suitable employment - now all is well. One son now head of pathology at large state hospital, other son is property tax consultant. Both have married and have own families now.

My economic situation is probably better now than if I had stayed in Rhodesia because I receive a pension in sterling. However my standard of housing has never remotely approached that which I had in Rhodesia. Our children have both graduated from prestigious universities in the United Kingdom which they may not have done had we remained in Rhodesia.

I am constantly amazed that Rhodesia was so advanced in so many administrative areas compared to United Kingdom e.g., planning, road signs, traffic control, municipal services, availability to the rate payers and personal accountability.

I have had a good and full life. Became a city councillor and have had many other positions. Am currently church elder. I love Zimbabwe and wish her well, enjoy going back but my place in the world is now the Netherlands.

Prefer to be associated with Zimbabwe rather than Rhodesia as former is often indicative of more racially tolerant people than the latter - I enjoyed life in Rhodesia but grew with and accepted need for change and worked for reconciliation. There were many injustices on both sides in the war as there always are. I miss the friends who fought and died for the wrong reasons but I do like to keep contact with people from pre-independence days (1980). I left for economic reasons and to provide a future for my daughter. Had I been single without a child I would have stayed probably a lot longer but perhaps not forever. I lived 3 years in Canada, before Australia and am not sure whether I should have stayed there.

In retrospect education at private school in Zimbabwe would have been preferable to govt. education in RSA. Eldest son settled in United Kingdom says "you can keep Africa". Other 2 children still hanging around. Still miss easy going people in Zimbabwe - RSA not so friendly. can see no long term future here - would have been better to have gone straight out of Africa. However age now against us. Rhodesians now known as herewes - here we go again!

I will NEVER understand why foreign aid at the expense of the British taxpayer is poured into third world countries only to be squandered or misdirected into the hands of those countries leaders and western leaders must know this - but do nothing about it. I also receive govt. pension but see the value of R$ so it's not worth much and I have capital in Zimbabwe which is virtually worthless.

Our main objective to educate our children at the best level was achieved. This was confirmed when we visited Zimbabwe in 94 and saw the current standard of education. A small consolation for leaving that wonderful country. If financially possible we would retire there tomorrow.

I have adapted well into the countries of my choice after leaving Rhodesia/ Zimbabwe, South Africa and now Auckland - that is in the physical sense. Mentally it is a lot harder to come to terms with such an enormous upheaval - tearing up roots that one thought were in the ground for ever. The break up of our social structure, the dispersal of family and friends - a shattering experience - one I am only now recovering from having been back to Zimbabwe 4 years ago to lay the ghost.

If the situation in Zimbabwe were to improve and whites were wanted there again my wife and I would return even though we have achieved well here and run my own business.

Many young men had their lives turned upside down because of UDI and a lot of people lost loved ones through UDI and a lot of people had to start new live sin strange countries from square one again. Start new jobs and different works with many different people from other parts of the world.

Twenty years after I left school I founded an association for Hamilton Old Boys and held a series of reunions in 5 cities. I have met at least 600 pupils/staff and established many friendships as a result.

My ex husband was a mine manager in Rhodesia. When we went on holiday and left the house open we just told the house boy when we would be back and we never found anything stolen. Here in South Africa you can't even leave your door open while you hang washing on the line without fear of finding someone waiting inside for you on your return. You have to be locked in all the time.

Some times I get really depressed when I think of friends all over the world - brother could not settle here and moved to Botswana near Zimbabwe border.

While it was difficult to get going in a strange country it was good to be without financial restrictions. I believe that if the situation had not changed in 79/80 I would probably never have left the Air Force since I was quite happy with the way of life. However honest hard work has now led me to a better life and most certainly a far higher position in business life that was self taught in order to move ahead in a strange country.

What upsets me most is that my mum and step dads pension has been cut to a ridiculous amount due to devaluation of the Z$ (she lives in SA). She cannot migrate to Australia because the govt. take into account all children from previous marriages (3 in United Kingdom, 1 in New Zealand, 1 in South Africa, 1 in Zimbabwe, 1 in Australia). So many families have been split and planted all over the world when young families should have full support from parents and grand parents to teach real values and how to live properly. Grandparents are so important.

Many "innovations" in South Africa have a Rhodesian behind them some where. Since the elections there has been far less bitterness towards the "whenwes" in South Africa.

The first 2 weeks were spent watching political party conferences on TV! However much I disagreed with what I heard I was over-awed by the political freedom and realities that these conferences exemplified. The first realization that we weren't as perfect as I though we were.

Here because my wife is a Scot. Bloody awful climate.

Born of British parents in South Africa. Lived in Bechuanaland but brought up in Rhodesia. Although I've lived longer in Australia than Rhodesia I still describe myself as a Rhodesian. After nearly 3 decades in Australia I am almost settled - however Africa will always be in my blood.

Now that my wife and I have retired we propose to join our children in Australia - say good-bye to Africa for the last time. We are not prepared to go through another Rhodesia in RSA at our age.

Since leaving Rhodesia myself and my family have moved closer to the Lord.

The best 8 years of our lives were those we spent in Rhodesia. The children have all been back and one is still there. Even the riots at the university had their moments - the chanting was good-natured and lacked menace.

After the bush war a black said to me "You whites were too soft on us blacks". On interrogating an educated, captured gook he said his men avoided old men in short camo pants like me (as I was dressed at the time - 42 years old) as they were very vigilant. He told me of a time he hid in a mango tree while a black soldier smoked a cigarette below him before being uplifted by chopper. Assisted in relocation of 36 black rhino as reintroduction to Gona re Zhou in 71. Photographed cows with calves in 1976. Reputed population up to 150 by 91. Authorities moved rhino out in 93 but only 3 were found. So much for Zimbabwean conservation. Game rangers themselves were responsible according to friends still in the business.

At time of arrival in United Kingdom (March 79) RW did not exist and we knew no other Rhodesians in the area we settled in. Local people had no conception of our feelings, our desperation etc. My wife's non-Rhodesian relations in Scotland were very supportive albeit from a distance.

UDI was an ill-timed act of monumental folly which lead directly to the entrenching in power of a corrupt, incompetent, Marxist terrorist regime in what was once a wonderful country. The perpetrators achieved in fact precisely the opposite of what they intended and this was obvious at the time UDI was being contemplated.

When I stopped trying to retain aspects of my Rhodesian lifestyle I found it easier to settle down in my new country.

Rhodesians are the second "Jewish" race in that there is a coun try to which they should belong but circumstances have forced them to reside worldwide. They endeavour to instill in their children the respect, culture and attitude that man's moral fibre should attain to but alas all remain "children of the universe" in a strange, perplexing, non tangible brotherhood. Are we the lost race?

In Johannesburg we recognize the Rhodie Mafia - one finds old Rhodie achievers everywhere and doors open to one of the tried and tested.

Although we didn't take too well to the United Kingdom it was very good to us in that we arrived with nothing and were able to get back on our feet and provide for our retirement in a dozen years. I spent 20 years in the BSAP Reserve mainly in PATU. I experienced the best and worst of times. I miss it all - the whites and blacks. I was fortunate to have had so many wonderful African years. We are proud to still call ourselves Rhodesians.

Arrived in United Kingdom in Jan 71. Became head of school after 5 years.

Concerns re education and value system in Canada. Have done well financially but still feel disorientated and displaced here. Within days of returning to Zimbabwe felt at home despite changes the feeling of home is till there. Immediate rapport with others Rhodies in Canada despite differences in circumstances and experiences. Can't believe how many comments from other Rhodies re inability to settle. the lost tribe is a large nomadic family. It seems many of us have difficulty settling elsewhere although many don't want to.

In spite of my acceptance of current living conditions the joy I experience on hearing a Rhodie accent and the discovery of more expatriates and their delight when I use a Rhodesian colloquialism - instant rapport. Both sons expert in Chilapapa agree with this wholeheartedly.

Although I have the veldt in my heart I do not believe I would be the person I am today if we had no left. I'm hoping to put roots down. The feeling of not truly belonging anywhere but in a place that has a different name and doesn't want me even though I was born there never really seems to go away. But I can go home to refuel my soul when needed.

Life has been good to us in Canada. Both my wife and I have achieved executive positions in banking.

No regret on life in Rhodesia which was "hairy" near the end as I was in Intaff and travelled in terrorist areas. It was however a fascinating life.

I would be interested to see the proportion of Rhodesians in age group 35-45 who feel UDI was good idea. We had no say in the decision yet bore its consequences in the bush war. Would be interesting to see some demographics on achievements, earnings, success as entrepreneurs, education standards etc. by Rhodesians c.f., western norms

Only problem is regular devaluation of Z$. When I left Zimbabwe in 83 my contributed pension was £500 p.m. Today I receive £75 and have to receive aid from UK govt. which is embarrassing but feel that if the United Kingdom hadn't enforced changeover so rapidly the country could have become one of the greatest and most peaceful in Africa

Travelled 6500 miles across world to meet up with RW purely by accident and have met more ex-Rhodesians, both old friends and new acquaintances and feel more "at home" now than in last 15 years. Also contacted ex-colleague after 20 years of lost ties.

We have spent the last 8 years improving our economic status. My wife is a graduate member of Institute of Credit Management. I recently completed an MBA with University of East Anglia. To ensure best education possible within our means we sent our son to a selective grammar school.

Drove across Canada in 81 to new job in BC. Economy collapsed late 81. Abandoned wife and 3 children to return to South Africa on last $. Had job offer in Joburg in 2 weeks. Wife and family managed to save fares to South Africa and shipped Rhodesian furniture to South Africa. Arrived 9 months later to immediate jobs and good schooling for youngster. After 13 years hard work retired in Cape Garden route area to embark on B and B project in beautiful and happy surroundings.

Being Rhodesian creates a feeling of envy in some South Africans. They appear to look up to us and expect more from us. Few of the whites in Zimbabwe appear to have that certain "something" that once identified a Rhodesian. Perhaps this is because they have been overwhelmed by expats and you rarely see a true Rhodesian any more.

Of all the other nationals I have met in the past 5 years Rhodesians retain their national identity the most and seem keen to keep the spirit of UDI alive. Although we have been scattered we have not been defeated.

We must stick together and plan and organize to reclaim our country which was stolen from us!

Wife always refused to visit Zimbabwe since she left in 79. Finally she had to go on business and thoroughly enjoyed it and now misses her homeland. Lost all our pension and most life insurances. Hope now to retain good health to work even part time as many years as possible.

I left Zimbabwe when I was 17 with my parents for South Africa. I married and divorced a fellow Rhodesian. I lived in South Africa for 9 years and hated the place -especially the politics. Emigrated to Australia, remarried and have 2 more children. We love Australia. It is country of great opportunity for emigrants who are prepared to work at anything. I would love my husband and children to see Rhodesia (Zim) before it is totally ruined and all wild life exterminated.

Have lost contact with friends. Hope to go for holiday next year - you never know I may be able to stay.

Reason for leaving was to give 2 daughters a secure future, more friends and structured life. That has been achieved.

March with other Rhodesians in Sydney on Anzac day.

Leaving was tough but inevitable. The magic of the way of life in Rhodesia did not prepare me for the facts of life of settling in Australia. However we contacted the Good Neighbours Council in Brisbane. The manager was trained in the Empire Flying scheme in Rhodesia. He contacted a fellow Air Force bloke (also trained in Rhodesia) who ran a migrant hostel and allowed us to stay there although we were not entitled. This saved us as our meager funds would have been used on accommodation in about a week.

Tain't the same in Africa. I miss the warmth/friendliness of the Shona/Ndebele people and the msasa trees. Rhodesian beef too. But we retain a good standard of living in South Africa and have accepted changing ways - mainly because of our incontrovertible belief in the lord - but we'd like to settle in the United Kingdom if possible.

Born Insiza 1914. Both parents early settlers, owned estate in Insiza district at Fort Rixon. Attended boarding school at Bulawayo then Milton. Joined BSAP in 32 serving 3 years then went to Kitwe Copper, leaving in 39 for Kenya to join Kenya Regiment and served with KAR. On discharge in 46 in Salisbury worked for Escom from whom I took pension and left for New Zealand.

Pursued highly successful career selling insurance. Training in being MIC of BSAP stations proved a sold foundation in self-discipline. I owe most of my achievement since leaving Rhodesia to the traditions and character building of the BSAP.

Have retained close Rhodesian friends and ties. We will always treasure our Rhodesian years. We had our children there, married and had many happy years. We leave family ashes there sadly.

Zimbabwe is beginning to appreciate there is much to be learned both positive and negative from its past. I intend to return home in the next 2 years. My work is most of my life and here it is not worth living in the (dis)organizational culture of this workplace.

It is a good feeling to meet other Rhodesians and talk about the old days but we must look to the future - life goes on.

We stayed on board ship for many years. Now we have left we see how poorly things really are in Zimbabwe, especially with regards to personal safety and law and order. If there were responsible government, law and order and a promising economic future we would choose Zimbabwe. However New Zealand is a wonderful country and things have gone really well for us here. We could, of course, take so much with us now.

We find New Zealand are just like the old Rhodesians - they just talk funny. Many older associates in Zimbabwe stated before we left "Kiwis were the finest chaps we met in the 39-45 war" and we now understand and appreciate that statement as we have settled very well close to 50% of our family. New Zealand is the world's best kept secret in our opinion.

I left Rhodesia as a teenager having been born there but lived mainly in South Africa. Most of my relatives are now in South Africa or UK. We lived and worked in Zambia for 2 years at time of UDI so we felt its affects. It didn't affect our love of the country and ordinary folk. If ONLY the Federation hadn't been forced on us we'd still be there...maybe.

Arrived in New Zealand with $80, no job, no accommodation and 2 children. An ex-Rhodesian family shared their home with us for 3 weeks. Wife started work within 2 weeks and I 2 weeks later. Both on fairly low incomes. As I had no assets or track record I had to take out large insurance policy and this coupled with repayment of 2 loans accounted for entire month' salary. For 3½ years we battled on my wife's salary. Only 1 uniform each for the children and no funds for extra mural activities. We led a Spartan existence. Later we were both promoted. We continued a modified Spartan existence to ensure a modest but comfortable retirement. We achieved this in 8½ heartbreaking but satisfying years.

Its good to drive without convoys, land mines etc. to have a choice of articles to buy. I miss Africa very much. Trying to sort out my late husband's affairs in Zimbabwe is a nightmare - inefficiency of government depts. Mail not answered etc.

As a journalist I covered most of the terrorist war. I knew much of what was going on and that South Africa would betray Rhodesia. When my employer was murdered by terrorists I returned to England. His death made up my mind to get out. I would not work for an indigenous government now riddled with corruption with the rich getting richer. I am proud of the professional job I did in Rhodesia. Now grateful to be in UK. Truth in Zimbabwe being ignored and not published in West.

I'll never stop being a Rhodesian and cherish the memories of friends of that time. However I've also grown a lot in strength and understanding and within myself as a result of my life experiences.

Living in United Kingdom has been more difficult than normal because local authority allowed expansion of haulage/ warehousing business to come so close to our property as to seriously affect our lives and value of property which is subject to much low frequency noise at night. Locked in dispute with council plus parochial attitude which is beyond belief and borders on chauvinism. It has affected our health and we are restricted in our options by modest incomes.

Being born and raised in Rhodesia and coming to terms with move to United Kingdom has made me a much stronger person able to cope with anything. My husband came with me to Rhodesia/Zimbabwe on holiday and we feel we would like to move back there. Obviously with the economic situation we intend to ensure financial security.

Arrived in 76 and worked as coal delivery person, foundry worker, pioneer concrete rep and then I bought a bakery which was successful until recession and could not survive with multiples. Am now allowed back as bakery consultant in Zimbabwe on 1 year contract provided I take in Z$500,000 with no security.

Since returning to United Kingdom I can honestly say I have never felt so insecure before in my life. Age seems to be the be all and end all of everything. Perhaps my feelings are due in part to the fact I am single. I shared my house with a fellow ex-Rhodesian for financial reasons. He passed away so I now feel lost.

When I remarried unexpectedly I was able to give my little terrace house to my daughter which enabled her to join me in England and have her own home.

I ran the catering at Pinewood Film studios for 7 years very successfully. Rubbed shoulders with all the stars etc. Too many incidents to record. I am now within the NHS having commissioned and opened a new catering concept.

On has to accept that Rhodesia is no more. I grew up in a peaceful country but Africa throughout has retrogressed and life is cheap there. the violence in South Africa is appalling and unacceptable and as a white person I tired of being blamed for the position blacks find themselves in. They blame everything on slavery/colonialism/apartheid but never look to themselves for the solution - they want everything for nothing and I'm not interested in people who take and destroy. The average black wants peace - he will have to work.

I found at my age settling in the United Kingdom horrendous and would not advise any Rhodesian to do it.

Came to Rhodesia in 63 with wife and 2 kids from United Kingdom. Had good job in United Kingdom but was fed up with unions etc. Rhodesia at that time was in rough period after Federation but still land of opportunity. Became first white van salesman (ice cream) in Rhodesia. Lowest paid member of DMB, when I joined. I earned 2½% commission and £50 p.m. with graft, long hours. In just over a year earned more than the dairy manager. Took 15 years to get from bottom to top in sales. I loved Rhodesia, memories.

Rhodesia as a country was not unique but Rhodesians were and are. The nearest I've got to their friendliness and open nature is meeting with some kiwi Lions at a convention in Tokyo. The sad thing that has to be faced that when our generation passes away so does this uniqueness which was rooted in the land, climate and its diverse peoples.

Major achievement is that we have been able to pick threads of a normal life again. we have learned during the years of living in England that the image of English people as being a gentle and cultured race is false. The country is riddled with double standards. Having made these comments there are some decent people about but they take some finding.

Although not born in Rhodesia still consider Bulawayo my home. My only regret is that I was too young to fight in the war. However Rhodesia is gone and we must look to future. In Zimbabwe most have integrated well but some of the ex-Rhodies living elsewhere are still living in the past. I attended a RW function. All the 400 people there were white. This disturbed me but in retro spect I should have expected it. I go back to Bulawayo as often as possible but that is Zimbabwe now and I have to adapt and integrate.

I joined the Police Reserve in Centenary during war and served 7 years. On moving to Scotland I looked for work and told Boots I worked for Barbours in Salisbury as cosmetics consultant. They believed me and ,starting work the next week, found the girl next to me was from Bulawayo. I worked for 5 years and attended all the training sessions. It was difficult leaving a 2000 acre farm in Centenary for Scotland with 3 children and no home. Now I don't regret it at all having been back to Zimbabwe to look.

We were both in ours 20s when we moved there and found relatively easy to settle back except for lousy climate. Two daughters found it much harder to settle out of Rhodesia.

In common with many other ex-Rhodies we know we have really made headway since becoming self employed. United Kingdom is great for many things but we miss the climate. Hence we have just bought a condo in the Algarve - ready for retirement.

Southern Rhodesia was a wonderful country, especially prior to 1940. Changed for worse when RAF training scheme arrived and again after arrival of immigrants for post war settlement. Federation, abolition of common voters roll and lastly UDI and civil war completely destroyed much of what was best about pre-war (1940) SR. The happy days are gone for ever but the memory remains.

I am proud to have achieved a BA (Hons) with the Open University.

Bought a mobile home in Cornwall very close to Rhodesian friends. Then moved to daughter who decided they couldn't stand UK climate and moved to Australia. Having been brought up in Dr. Barnardo's foster home feel rather lonesome at times.

Feel very alone. We had 2 sons born in Rhodesia. One died. Younger son in Harare so have no relatives here. Went to Rhodesia in 38, joined Nursing Service during war. Went onto 3000 acres of virgin land, lived in pole and dagga in 47. Left 4 bed, 2 bath house with cottage, pool and tennis court in 76. I believe it is pitiful sight - the house only a shell.

As a Rhodesian and former hockey international am proud to be employed by Daily and Sunday Telegraph (London) and despite my accent I do a lot of work for BBC radio, BBC World service and odd documentary programs for TV. I worked for BBC at the Seoul and Barcelona Olympics and travel the world - such opportunities simply wouldn't exist in Zimbabwe.

Found going to South Africa traumatic. In general people didn't like Rhodesians - they resented us because we took over jobs they wanted. After loosing insurances in Rhodesia when we left we decided not be caught again in South Africa with the result that when made redundant we only had very small pension hence our move to United Kingdom where we got income support and free medical. Otherwise we would have been beggars. If we had work offered and a place to live we would very much like to return to Rhodesia/Zimbabwe.

When I arrived in the United Kingdom my attitude was knowing I had to adjust fast to survive. Worked very hard and without a diploma in my industry have made it to manager of the business I run. I had to focus on what I knew I needed to get where I am today.

Brief periods of unemployment, variety of jobs, production car worker, accounts assistant, auto lathe setter, milkman, lorry driver - now markets manager of city markets.

I get some racial verbal attacks from blacks when they find out I'm Rhodesian.

When people ask where I am from and I say Zimbabwe they think for a while and then say "Oh, you mean Rhodesia" and I just nod and smile.

The political situation in United Kingdom is making me think very hard about returning to Zimbabwe.

When and where possible I do volunteer hospital and hospice duties. Would do more but am not allowed to work as I'm on income support.

Lack of funds due to massive deterioration of my Zimbabwe pension - now £1 for Z$12 and the utter refusal of Mugabe government to rectify a moral responsibility.

Despite the years that have passed I still miss Rhodesia and despite the war had a unique childhood. Rhodesia played a huge part in my formative years - I think I was very fortunate.

My wife and I were recruited in Zimbabwe by National Trust as a consequence of work in theatre to administer a theatrical museum and private theatre. We have 8 years to the end of the contract thus our difficulties in adapting to another country were not great.

My wife and I are both teachers so had enough income to buy a house with large mortgage and also fund 3 children to go to university. We also enjoy a reasonable standard of living and take advantage of the great wealth of entertainment and culture in London. As teachers in Zimbabwe we could not have afforded tertiary education in South Africa for our family.

I also received considerable abuse from pensioners when they discovered I had come from Rhodesia and had no pension.

My life in Rhodesia was happy and I have many memories but sadly that is all they are. My hope is to return one day.

Apart from the recession and employment problems I have settled well in Great Britain. Our jobs are stable. If possible I would consider moving to another country as I enjoy travelling.

Without relatives in Australia our move would have been much harder and would have stopped in South Africa except I realized it would go same way. One's heart is where one spends one's youth, then where the family were born. My biggest regret is my children will not experience the Rhodesia I knew - the bush, the old garden "boy", kaffir paths, strange fruits, mahobohobo etc. To awake before dawn with the smell of the dew on the winter grass.

When I went to present for a "living" people expected a black person as if only blacks live in Africa. Have been able to make parishioners aware of problems of Africa and make them thankful for what they have.

Severe medical problem helped by NHS - would not have been available in Zimbabwe.

In its way UDI was a success. It made Rhodesians proud to be Rhodesians, created a spirit of togetherness, created initiative in technical matters. It would have been a wholesale success without interference from the rest of the world, that slob Kissinger and the let down by RSA. Ian Smith was right in what he did and were history to repeat itself I would back him all the way.

I found people here completely disinterested in the fact that I was a newcomer and that I needed friendship etc. to settle down. People here are egocentric and uncaring in the main.

Although both British by birth we could not settle in the UK, felt out of place and nothing in common with people. However here in Spain we have a lot in common with the mostly well travelled, cosmopolitan, ex-pat community and the life style, weather and flora (not fauna) are just the same as Rhodesia.

It is a crying shame that a wonderful people are now scattered round the globe never to be brought together again. I miss people who speak their mind at any costs, seldom hold a grudge for long and who show genuine friendship.

Achieved ambition to become fast jet pilot with RAF but missed the Gulf war by a couple of years.

Having emigrated from what became an alien country in which I was born of Pioneer stock (1895 Steyn Trek) I try to make the best of it. However my wife makes it easier - she is proudly Rhodesian by marriage and we celebrated our golden wedding in 95. She thinks like a Rhodesian (not a little old English lady) and spent more years in England than out of it.

I always find it amusing to hear the difference in our every day language compared to the "poms". We call a traffic light a robot. Road circle - roundabout, chips - crisps, packet - bag and the favourite "just now" - the poms think this is within a couple of minutes and cannot comprehend what we mean. It takes many years to talk like a pom.

I still hate the UK climate and find living hard physically - part due to age and health problems. Living in a small house I now find the people more friendly but still have to be careful not to seem nosy by expressing interest in them. I worry about future for elderly when less help seems available and affordable retirement homes cannot compare to those in Zimbabwe.

Father joined Paulings and surveyed most of railway lines to Bulawayo, fought at Mafeking. Surveyed line from Beira to Salisbury. Discovered line to Old Umtali was impossible. Was captain in Nyasaland Mechanical Transport i/c Fort Johnstone in 1914-18. I was first horticulturist to form a dept. in Rhodesia Railways.

Hardest task was to make people understand the difference between South Africa and Rhodesia and also that the accent was not Australian.

I still love that country.

I made it in South Africa through tenacity, hard work, inventiveness, seizing opportunities, open mindedness, being friendly and inviting(made it to top of large national company). Today I own 2 businesses. My attitudes are no different to most Rhodesians of my era. We believe no one and no place owes us anything. We merely do it to the best of our ability and reap the just rewards fairly and squarely. Rhodesians are a special people and were molded by special circumstances wherever they are. They can do and be anything they want.

My children have had a better education than Zimbabwe could provide. They took up the challenge and all achieved well. Daughter was Rotary exchange student, son captained U19 Eastern Province side. I have to work much harder than Rhodesian days but earn well, have a good standard of living travel overseas annually.

Opened retail chemist from scratch at age 51. Worked 70 hours p.w. including public holidays for 6 years. Sold business at good price. Health suffering from hassles from drug addicts, physically threatened 10 times, spat at. Two burglaries, one armed holdup but fought back and overpowered masked man. He got 18 mths. and was HIV+. Had South African bastard written in lipstick on shop window. I'm OK but you should see the other guy.

All my ex-Rhodie friends I think still have great strength of character, a great sense of style but still fairly gentle. Achievements include playing with some of world's top orchestras. Just had No.1 hit in UK charts with band I play with. I and other Rhodie were youngest ever to graduate from Royal College of Music.

Awarded meritorious service medal in 79 for service in operational areas while in Lands Inspectorate.

Major problems solved when found employment as domestics in large country house. How could senior civil servants do this? Easy. Apply your expectations of those who once worked for you to yourself and ensure you achieve standards expected of others. Hard work but rewarding and gave most interesting insight to vastly different ways of life. We saved enough to buy mobile home until devaluation of Z$ caused us to sell it and move into 1 bed flat owned by charitable organization.

Circumstances frequently dictate the paths our lives take. Politics/independence plus a divorce brought me back to the UK, but for these would probably still be in Rhodesia but in all fairness I must admit the United Kingdom has been good to me with my children all here now but we will love Rhodesia for ever

I am appalled by hypocrisy and bigotry of minority groups in this country and the power they have in government i.e., ethnic minorities, gays militant feminists. If you are a white male of English background born in southern Africa you've really got a problem fitting in with the politically correct clowns that rule the roost. I feel sorry for white indigenous Europeans - especially decent English people not yobs, lefties etc.

It took me 13 years to get a permanent post in the teaching profession. I was kept on day supply and given short temporary contracts for years. I retrained as a state general nurse only to find no jobs available when I qualified so I returned to supply teaching. I often felt I was being discriminated against as I was a "white African" and not a black. I maintained my sanity in the early days as an émigré be keeping in contact with my friends overseas - without that and some reunions I would not have stayed sane.

Successful wild life artist for many years. Sold paintings all over world. One of Kandahar Island hangs in Victoria Falls hotel dining room an elephant painting in Gwai River Hotel. Bishop Muzorewa bought one of my elephant paintings. Because of my love for elephants Chief Chundu in Urungwe bestowed on me the honour of being the third white woman to attend the calling up of the spirit of Chimombe (during the war). People came from miles around to attend. During ceremony the spirits told me I would never be touched by "insects" (terrorists) and that certainly proved true. Many times places were attacked after I had passed through which didn't exactly make me a popular visitor. Had many requests to join me on various trips. Coincidence? I think I saw the best and the last of Africa. Africa still won't let me go. Would love to return to paint.

Rhodesians interact better with third world nationals, are more honest and hard working. The West are really a bunch of hypocritical racists.

Working at very permissive private prep school. Education lacks all the good educational principles we took for granted in Rhodesia. Our colleagues are unfailingly malicious about "those who lived so comfortably in the exploited colonies". We keep very quiet and miss the sane lifestyle we loved in Rhodesia.

Husband and I arrived at Heathrow with our clothes and me 33 weeks pregnant. No money to speak of. Years on we own a 4 bed detached house, owe no money, have 2 healthy normal children - all through hard work and determination. Husband in British Army - Major in Infantry with service in many countries.

Managed to find sheltered accommodation near one son but cannot fund our own home in area where can assimilate with like minded neighbours. Otherwise have managed regular trips to Europe and returned to Zimbabwe on 3 occasions. Have contact with several ex-Rhodesians.

Have established a rewarding career in Europe. Wife is ordained Anglican priest and has worthwhile occupation. Daughter received excellent education

Despite medical problems and although it is difficult making a new life at 61 I'm glad I came back now instead of 65. My children are in the United Kingdom but don't see them often.

Strong Rhodesian $ in 76 - we were very lucky.

My previous employer (daily newspaper) before emigration to Rhodesia offered me a staff job within 1 month of my return and, starting, from the bottom again I quickly worked my way up to a higher position than I held before leaving the paper in 72.

I find everything strange here and would dearly love to live back in Rhodesia/ Zimbabwe but could not afford to so I am grateful to the government and local council here.

In the anniversary celebrations of the war years no mention is made of the Rhodesians who gave their lives and who volunteered to fight for England. Rhodesia supplied the highest proportion of men from any commonwealth country. It is as if Rhodesia never existed - it is a never never land.

Since starting work both my wife and I have achieved senior positions in our employment through hard work. We sometimes find attitudes hard to understand but after 11 years are gradually being accepted.

I enjoyed my time in Rhodesia. My sons received good basic education which they built on. I was extremely impressed with the management training facility available in Salisbury and the highly motivated people (black and white) who took advantage of them.

Being invited to attend interviews when they had no intention of considering me for the job. They were more interested about my life in Rhodesia and Zimbabwe and not my qualifications.

Returned to South Africa to start own business for 5 years but left for United Kingdom again because of security.

I found the move to the United Kingdom gave me opportunities to develop as a person in my own right, go to night school, develop in business etc. which I wouldn't have been in Zimbabwe but sense of humour is necessary for survival.

On arrival in United Kingdom in 73 I had no job and family was split 3 ways but when I went to DHSS for help they told me to consider myself lucky to be there. I asked if I could get help if I blacked up and was evicted by the manager. I can't make up my mind whether we or the United Kingdom have changed but I find everyone so lazy, not wanting to help themselves and young women now just drop babies and say "What is the government going to do about it?". Then they get free housing and benefits. Old people seem forgotten.

Wife trained at Bulawayo Teachers College in 69 under auspices of University of London. They refused to acknowledge connection. After months of determination on her part including seeing MP she was allowed to teach and had to do probation. They have 2 categories EC and non EC trained. System does not cater for British trained overseas.

I retired from the Air Force after 20 years and became deputy chief security officer for a Municipality consisting of 250 personnel. I became chief security officer and the complement became 1500 - mostly ex-combatants. In spite of considerable political pressure and nepotism it worked. Earned a Brigadier's salary and wore fancy uniform but wife needed 2 knee joint replacements. This was done and she is now in good health.

Have become very involved member of community and made many friends including several Rhodesians.

Felt far more settled long term in United Kingdom than in Rhodesia/Zimbabwe. Have been back since and still feel we made the right decision.

We have suffered a great let down by Brit. government which is determined to regard us still as outlaws. Their attitude regarding the plight of Rhodesian pensioners is disgraceful.

We fly a Rhodesian flag on our narrow boat home which helps in recognition. We don't appreciate strong whenwe attitudes but find most ex-Rhodesians proud of their background without allowing it to hinder their new life.

At 81 I am glad to be back to my roots but miss Rhodesia. One son there keeps me in touch and an excuse to return. Brothers and sisters helped our return.

Main problem settling in was no children - they help you find friends - parents of their friends etc. Then getting used to UK climate. Enjoyed snow first winter.

We returned to Zimbabwe on 2 occasions after job offers - for 9 months and then for 5 years before retiring to South Africa. We were unhappy on the first occasion but settled well on the second and employed our old house servant from Rhodesian years who turned up having heard of our return on the bush telegraph.

You never fully appreciate Rhodesia/Zimbabwe until you are deprived of it.

What I miss more than anything is my work in southern Africa as a sports administrator.

We went to Rhodesia full of altruism and idealism to build a mighty new British dominion there. It is heart breaking that this ambition was not realized and brought to fulfillment.

Fortunately I found employment and the means to pay off a house. Present circumstances better than expected. Finances in future likely to be difficult. Early time in England easier with annuity from Zimbabwe but devaluation made nonsense of plans.

Leaving Zimbabwe was a traumatic experience. A close family circle was broken with loved ones spread around the world and our way of life gone for ever.

Will never forget Rhodesia and all it meant to my family but we have to move on and adapt.

Indigenous British are unable to differentiate between Rhodesia and South Africa. In many cases they were unaware of where Rhodesia was. On arrival took family to Harrods where children visited toy dept. On descending our 4 year old was faced by an

African 4 year old with toy rifle. Ours had hysterics and Harrods rang to cries of "terrorists".

The big problem in seeking employment in United Kingdom was that few could differentiate between Zimbabwe and South Africa and South Africa at that time was an international pariah and subject to sanctions. Once in employment I had little difficulty in persuading my employer to recruit one ex-Rhodesian in a professional capacity and one in a secretarial capacity .

It has been a huge struggle. We arrived in the United Kingdom with 4 suitcases, £500 and 2 small children. The job we were supposed to come to fell through. The first 2 years we just survived. We lost our pensions, insurance policies and it has been a struggle to establish a home. We also feel we don't belong either in the United Kingdom or Rhodesia anymore. In retrospect the whole episode was a nightmare. We were victims of history.

I remain bitter that we were virtually forced to leave a wonderful Rhodesia, where friendship and tolerance and not racism existed. World politics sold us down the river but I could never now return.

Went there as mature adults and enjoyed 19 years. Annoying that Z$ has lost value against £. My pension has decreased by 4-5 times.

After years of building up a pension for retirement I am a little bitter at rate of exchange especially as United Kingdom encouraged folks to go to commonwealth countries after 39-45 war.

Since being in Northern Ireland we have made many friends who have been wonderful in making us feel welcome. We have also been out and about to see many places. Everything is beautiful, scenery, people, towns and cities. I love Irish folklore and the great sense of humour the Irish have.

Although I got over the blues and got on with the business of living I have never got Rhodesia out of my system and am seriously thinking of retiring there.

Having worked out a deal with the Zimbabwe government the UK government will do nothing to get the release of our blocked funds. Yet they still pump aid into Zimbabwe.

Don't ever forget Rhodesia but don't become a whenwe. Be like an elephant "never forget". I found a boss who lived in South Africa so we talk the same lingo without translating all the time.

Had holiday in Zimbabwe over Xmas. Fantastic time - first visit in 8 years. Nothing much seems to have changed but Harare and Bulawayo looking very old and tired. Buildings need much work and black population very much more than before - too much.

Arrived with only household effects and holiday allowance. Found employment in bakery. Promoted after 6 months. Lived in rented accommodation 15 months. Found house at reasonable price. Paid off 15 year mortgage in 8 years. Miss working and salary. Rhodesian pension a write off due to devaluation. UK pension is small due to short period of residence but will manage with God's help.

In 1981 Zimbabwe government did not pay me for 3 months - then paid wrong amount . I still have not had a P6. We returned on the Achille Lauro which was impounded at Tenerife. After 3 days we were flown onto London and stranded there about 1 a.m. without accommodation in January. Rail strike in Zimbabwe - rail strike in UK.

Both wife and I found appropriate employment and we were able to plan for comfortable retirement after about 15 years even tough Rhodesian assets were frozen. 2 sons both university graduates, one engineer - other completing Ph.D. Will own own house in Oct this year. Disenchanted with Zimbabwe after holiday on account of security situation, inflation, unemployment, grubbiness. Realizing Zimbabwe assets a problem.

I learnt to be greatly self sufficient - able to do housework, laundry as well as cope with full time job. Became much less introspective and more positive and capable. Found that though the move was and still is painful it has been an immense and very successful character building exercise. This was my major achievement - especially to depend on myself and not servants etc.

Political detainee in Chikurubi for 2 years before emigrating.

Since leaving Zimbabwe in 86 my wife and I have moved on 12 occasions in most cases buying dilapidated properties, remodeling them and selling them. We now own 4 properties, 3 of which we rent plus our own home. We shall shortly sell this and move on.

Even after 29 years strangers who have been to Rhodesia/ Zimbabwe can still pick up my accent.

Youngest child gained considerably by completing high school and university in UK. Elder son adapted brilliantly to state system. He, wife and 3 children live solely on state benefits.

Daughter and Rhodesian born son in law employed and prospering but miss sunshine.

Our "garden boy" who I managed to get a job for in the Telecommunications Corp. has obtained a higher technicians certificate after more than 10 years home study. I feel very proud to have helped him in my small way.

Soon we hope to move to a housing association flat as I have to give up work. I regret leaving Rhodesia because of the developing situation at that time. I believe more could and should have been done to help those who chose to leave, specially financially.

Unable to obtain own accommodation. Lived with wife's mother. Financial restrictions. Wife worked since return to United Kingdom - no help in house. Narrow minded British who have never traveled or grasped current affairs in either United Kingdom or rest of world.

Six weeks after arriving in United Kingdom we were ready to call it a day here and return to Rhodesia (we had come with return tickets). However we were notified that our car and furniture were on the water and it was this reason only that made us stay. Fortunately life improved when our personal effects arrived and we acquired our own home. If it hadn't been for the car and furniture we would undoubtedly be in Zimbabwe today.

I am intensely proud of having been part of what was Rhodesia but no longer consider myself Rhodesian. This is not through any notions of "political correctness" I just believe that life moves on and so must we. I will never forget my heritage and wish my children could be brought up in a similar environment but that is no longer likely. I now consider the British Army (not

UK) to be the point of my allegiance, as it still largely embodies old fashioned standards.

Since leaving Rhodesia my health has deteriorated but I am assured of medication to alleviate problems (not always the case in Rhodesia - currency shortages). I am reading for a B.Sc. (Econ) at the Open University (excellent institution). Since retiring to the United Kingdom I have coped with 2 redundancies, 3½ years unemployment and 1½ years self-employment - financially disastrous but have also managed to design and build own house and make some good new friends.

Happiest days of my life were spent in Rhodesia. Only returned to United Kingdom for health reasons. Miss Rhodesian friends very much.

I thought I knew many Rhodesians yet am surprised in meeting so many through business, social contact now in the UK. Deduct the current population from the from the 1980 total and it is surely a tribe in considerable number that is spread world wide.

Wife has received her bus/train pass. People are friendly in the UK. Less chance of being robbed.

I am inclined to say UDI was a success as I would not have had the upbringing and education that I did or be part of the society I knew as Rhodesia if it had not happened. The Rhodesia I remember was forged from the pressures of UDI/the war, a real fighting people. But I am very saddened that good people died buying us those years - that is one aspect of being a Rhodesian I NEVER forget. I feel I owe it to those who did not make it to live my life to the full, positively as I have the opportunity to do.

More effort should be made to get the British government to compensate for financial losses suffered by the Lancaster House agreement such as savings and hard earned pensions which had already been worked for and paid for, saved for only to be handed over with insufficient thought commonsense and easy safeguards being applied. Our working lives were lost to us by British government's lack of loyalty to their own loyal kith and kin.

Consider myself lucky to have had 30 years in Rhodesia and that my children had the chance to grow up there.

Wish we had not come here and would not have done so if we had known the problems we were going to have for job, house etc. On the plus side my son would not have made it to university had we stayed. No use crying over spilt milk.

People have more often than not appreciated Rhodesia's resistance, in the past, to joining the rest of African nations in majority rule. However as times goes on less and less people have the guts to say what they mean in these days of political correctness. With South Africa now under black rule who will be the next - the UK?

This is not the England we left in 1948 - just like Zimbabwe is not the Rhodesia we went to, except they cannot alter the sunshine. The NHS is not what it is cracked up to be, nor is the pension payment. After doing 10 years in the forces and catching up as much as possible with contributions my OAP is only half. Very disillusioning, yet a slip of a girl on the bus with a 2 year old daughter blithely say she has a lovely flat with rent paid for her - no problems.

On reflection it was a great pity that white Rhodesians were so intolerant to change. The country was lost by their shortsightedness. This survey would not have been necessary if this had not happened.

At 78 I am somewhat soured off at the world I've returned to. Strange but I feel I have more in common with the Indian family (ex Kenya) running the local PO. Left with £5000 and 2 suitcases - less than I took out with me 38 years earlier. Have always been a spectator of life rather than an achiever.

We were lucky my father in law bought us a house so we had a roof over our heads. Our first Xmas was on folding chairs as we did not bring furniture with us. I got a job straight away and we got our 3 teenager daughters into school. They have all married English boys. The eldest and her husband are in mining and are happily settled in Johannesburg as no jobs exist for them here.

I had a wonderful working life - 3 years in Tanganyika, 2 years in India, 7 in England, 7 years in Rhodesia and 14 in South Africa and here no real gripes. However 3 British governments handed over with unseemly haste - Tanganyika, Rhodesia and South Africa to the black man. What a bloody record! Now they are doing their best to hand over Britain to the black man but fortunately it will take a few thousand years.

Living in the United Kingdom has been a big eye opener. It is totally different to what we were lead to believe. I would never again run down the African race as the British nation is morally and in a lot of cases has a lower standard of values than any African I know. If the opportunity arose to return to Zimbabwe I would be proud just to be African. I am a Zimbabwean now. I am far too ashamed to call myself English.

Moving is traumatic. It cannot be impulsive and requires long and careful planning. Stand up on your own 2 feet and think positive. Too many people rely on others.

We moved to United Kingdom in 85 till 87 when we returned to Zimbabwe hoping things would be better but found accommodation very hard to get and Z$ rates very low. So with health problems we returned to United Kingdom in 92. After death of my wife Wiltshire Council were very helpful in giving me a help line council flat which will help a lot. The only problem is that it is far from town centre and shops.

As a third generation Rhodesian it was a traumatic and heart rending decision to leave the country I loved and I still miss it very much. However the Rhodesia I knew has gone and one has to adapt and get on with life. I hope our history can somehow be preserved and the great achievements of the development of the country by the Europeans (irrespective of political and racial issues) will not be forgotten and ignored by historians.

We have concluded that if we didn't have children we would be in Zimbabwe, but feel that because of them they should grow up to know the ways of the world and not be isolated.

The decision to leave Zimbabwe was the worst I'm ever likely to make. It has irreparably damaged my marriage, isolated me from children and grandchildren. It was not an escape to a securer and better future as intended. In retrospect I should have stayed and done my bit to help the country I love to grow. Zimbabwean rules and finance prevent a return.

The British Government stated when they “took over” “legal” government from Rhodesia they would protect our pensions (recorded in Hansard). What protection? As retired Principal of the XX not one of the 25 odd lecturers I recruited from round the world are still in office and the multi racial classes I set up are a shadow of their former successes.

Born in Rhodesia, I left at 18 for university and worked in UK. Went back after 11 years. Retired to United Kingdom after 19 years. Got job as GP quickly. Fanatically determined to settle happily, despite being sole breadwinner. Husband English - born leader, difficulty in getting job but determined to settle though initially not happy. To settle happily in any other country, never ever be a "whenwe" and firmly refuse to yearn daily and audibly - virtually everyone got on a plane, train or boat voluntarily.

I am really battling to overcome the stigma of being classed a racist. I feel it has something to do with me being unable to find employment. A highlight while living in South Africa was joining Ian Smith, John Edmond and others at a Durban hotel to celebrate Rhodesia's "birthday". It brought back some wonderful memories and we met old friends again and shed more than one tear. The majority of our friends here and in South Africa are ex-Rhodies. We tend to stay friends for life. Rhodesians are a rare breed.

Maternal side of family were in Northern Rhodesia. Paternal side in Southern Rhodesia. All family eventually left Zambia for Rhodesia and South Africa and New Zealand. Family now resides mainly in South Africa. A few stayed in Zimbabwe. Family in New Zealand have now moved to Australia.

My children send me a ticket to South Africa every 2 years so I then visit Zimbabwe. I speak with many Africans I have known well. They have little hope for the future. The ordinary folk struggle to afford basics. I feel proud to have known and belonged to Rhodesia and only, feel sorry at the precipitous dissimulation of a people second to none. I blame the British government for badly handling the 1980 debacle which is the reason I did not retire to my roots.

As I get older and wiser I wish that we white Rhodesians had done more to help, educate and train black people. As I reflect on my own experiences from childhood through many years on a remote West Matabeleland cattle ranch I realize how dreadfully bad many of us were in the way we dealt with the black people. In many, many ways we Rhodesians got what was coming to us. Too many Rhodesians still talk as if it were the 1960s. So many Rhodesians here have not grown culturally, spiritually or emotionally and don't adapt more.

An English couple who met me and found where I was from were amazed to hear how well I spoke English and kept asking me to speak in my tribal dialect. They would not believe I had always spoken English in such a remote place.

Have 4 bed house, low mortgage, no debts, good health. Redundant twice, awful education system here, poor weather. Overall wish we had gone to Australia instead of England.

As almost the typical nuclear family we all felt the loss of Rhodesia deeply. But our youngest daughter suffered most - more than we realized. In fact with hindsight it is difficult to realize how one could take the step we did to leave (albeit the right decision intellectually). Fortunately our daughter overcame her early heartache but who knows at what psychological cost.

It seems to have added to a certain loss of identity - not to be recommended. I am now much more a pacifist - wars are lose-lose events.

Born of Pioneer stock and, together with my parents suffered innumerable hardships in striving to make Rhodesia into what it was at the time of handing over to Zimbabwe and remaining for a 3 year trial period I was not prepared to remain longer and witness the undoing of all the previous good work.

I love my Rhodesia and wish I had never had to leave. As in most cases we oldies could not live so far away from our young ones who had migrated earlier - so just had to follow.

Was sad to leave Rhodesia. Very happy there in both work and living. Have settled well in Australia. Would not go back now it is Zimbabwe. Have been back to see results of black rule.

All 5 children received university degrees. This was our aim in leaving Rhodesia as we were concerned at falling standards (and health and security) following independence in 1980. The children consider themselves Australian but I yearn for Rhodesia in the good old days.

I had to keep studying and now have a Ph.D. - the union ticket to work in the academic world. However this does not guarantee advancement to a high level as our accent and non-Australian background are a problem in a conservative field in which I work - agriculture. I work part time as a consultant overseas where I am better accepted and recognized. Still trying to find the right job back in Zimbabwe for a few years. Will definitely go back there to work if I find one next year.

When I first arrived in Bulawayo in 1948 I felt I had come home even though I did not know a soul apart from my husband and his sister. Rhodesia will always be home to me.

RAWA were very good to us when we arrived helping us make contact with other Rhodies, showing us round, loaning furniture to begin with.

Generally we have been very fortunate in our move and have settled very well in our new land. We have no regrets about leaving Rhodesia. We still hold Rhodesia as a special place in our hearts. We haven't looked back to our Rhodesian days but have looked forward into the future and have enjoyed the opportunities that Australia has offered to us.

There are now 17 ex-Rhodies in my retirement village near Perth. We are appreciated for the voluntary work we do and are very happy and active. In 77 and 78 we marched in the Anzac parade with the Australian Rhodesia association and carried the green and white flag. It then changed to the Rhodesian Association and we marched with the British ex-service league. In 94/95 I was in a bus as I cannot walk very far.

Now own 2 homes. 4 daughters all own their homes - top jobs. 2 have own business, 1 daughter is California. Husband has own business.

Amazed at lack of wildlife in rural areas. Cannot abide government that encourages low moral standards and fragmentation of family life. Basic foods contaminated with additives. Health care appears dependent on income despite Medicare. Drug treatments behind rest of world.

When we emigrated could not go back so had positive incentive to settle in. Making friends with native Australians has generally proved difficult and unrewarding. Have made most friends with new Australians, mainly ex-Africa. Now have some Australian friends who have moved interstate which has broadened their outlook.

I don't like Australia and would like to return to Europe, possibly Spain and work in the Middle East but have no desire to return to Zimbabwe.

My parents are both buried at Forest Hills outside Salisbury. I think that is why I will always consider Rhodesia home.

Generally I found the questionnaire negative and it fails to emphasize opportunities rather than problems or at least acknowledge that many Rhodesians have resettled and are highly successful and happy.

I was fortunate to find Australia. It is beautiful and user friendly. Maintained employment throughout the family. Eldest son in Air Force for 7 years, resigned and put himself through commercial pilots licence. Second son played rugby for western Australia and worked for Puma for 9 years. Third son qualified sky diving instructor. All very happy in Australia now

Went to Rhodesia from United Kingdom from 61-81. Emigrated to Australia to continue working in mining. Return regularly to Zimbabwe for business and friends. Still have frozen assets, future pension locked in so hope country remain viable. Race relations at grass roots level remain high in Zimbabwe and remain the best in the world despite all the hype from UK, USA and Australia.

Proud to have been an active part of the Rhodesian rebellion. Have 2 Rhodesian children doing well in Australia.

I was amazed how aware Australians were of having convict ancestors. Circumstances here and in the world have altered for the worse since I came here.

We have worked hard and Australia has been good to us.

We paid off our house after 12 years and sent our children to private schools after arriving in Australia in 81 with Z$1000. We both got jobs without problems and neither is a professional person.

In Australia my children obtained a good education and are both at university but I feel they missed out on a lot by not growing up in Rhodesia as it was. Both are keen to go to Zimbabwe on holiday.

Rhodesia was "Gods own country". My new home of Australia must be second on the list although it has taken many years to actually realize this - if only for the outback and many beauty spots. Don't care for cities which have become similar world wide.

I find clumps of Rhodesians or South Africans live in the past. I find their company boring and embarrassing. I loved my life in Rhodesia but it's gone and there is no use crying over spilt milk.

We spent 4 years in Perth working at any well paying job e.g., oil rigs off coast. 1985 bought a farm in Queensland where we grow roses and avocados. We ended up neighbours with our neighbours in Centenary.

Wife always wanted to return to Rhodesia until 1988 when we went to Harare to visit son and found how badly standards had fallen and how the city centre stank. She was happy to leave there and even happier to leave United Kingdom for Australia.

Have achieved more in 13 years in Australia than during 24 years in Rhodesia.

All Rhodesians I have come across have done reasonably well in their adapted countries. Because we have a good name for working hard, we also have integrity which we are respected for.

Our son and daughter are doing well here. We feel we cannot leave while they stay. In retrospect we feel we should have gone to the United Kingdom not Australia but its too late now.

Leaving Rhodesia and therefore not having to go into army and fight a war I did not believe in was the soundest decision I ever made. Looking back I am amazed how short a period Rhodesia existed for and how the world has passed by the era and values which "Rhodesia" stood for.

Emigration after 60 is a dodgy business even with close family ties in the country. It is particularly difficult as the previous country had so much going for it. My wife and I emigrated to Rhodesia - we were young and adaptable and had no wish to return to UK, even bringing my parents out to Rhodesia.

I own a business employing 5 Australians, own my own home and can travel - all achieved over 10 years - this I believe I could not have done in Rhodesia. It is only when pressed with the upheaval of moving to a new country that one is forced to get off one's ass and do something. This has made most Rhodesians successful. I don't think I would have done as much with my life had I stayed in Rhodesia.

Major achievement was being able to retire to United Kingdom with house, car all paid for and a reasonable standard of living. Worst thing was death of wife in car accident but this brought the family together and we have a very different outlook on life now.

Even today we still experience Anglo-Boer war when we are forced into contact with lower class of Afrikaner. By maintaining Rhodesian culture and standards we survive quite nicely. Son was headboy for school in 94 - mostly because of his strong Rhodesian base we have set for both our kids. We only let on we are Rhodesians when we are sure of our company as quite a few have blackened our name.

Being determined to build a new life, despite negativeness experienced and being accused of being a "whenwe". On the whole think ex-Rhodesians worked wonders in South Africa having arrived with very little - I had to start over again at 40.

It has been challenging - at times difficult but enormously rewarding in terms of personal and family growth. We are grateful to Rhodesia for our youth but not in the least maudlin about it. We wish Zimbabwe well and are proud to be called Rhodesians or Zimbabweans.

I'm glad we got the chance to begin again in Australia. We have been lucky and unlucky. I went back to school as a mature student and found the school kids and the Australian education better than the Salisbury Convent. I am happy and fortunate to live in Tasmania. I do miss the garden boy for the "sebenza" but

I'm glad not to have servants. Husband has missed the achievement of professional status he would have got in Rhodesia.

I still love Rhodesia/Zimbabwe and will continue to visit for as long as I can but much doubt I could afford to go back an live there. Am not unhappy in the United Kingdom but am pleased that I can visit South Africa and Zimbabwe regularly. You cannot shake the dust of Africa completely from between your toes.

Trying to master the meaning of Australian. When I started work I felt foolish because I had no idea how to work the office coffee machine - there are no "tea-boys" here.

I take great pride in being Rhodesian. I never miss an opportunity to tell people when introduced. Whenever challenged that it's now Zimbabwe I remind them that Mugabe changed the name - not me. It's on my citizenship and passport. I wear Rhodesian T-shirts. It was Rhodesia when I went there and it was Rhodesia when left.

Husband became director of company as he was in Rhodesia but it has been a long hard struggle as we never emigrated and had to start from scratch. Children have more opportunities than they had in Zimbabwe. We are freer with our money here but we do miss servants and pets.

We went to Holland in 84 (my wife is Dutch). After 2 years working hard we bought a bar and building and still work hard. Main problem is still the weather and lack of humour. For the rest Holland has been good but it is still a battle all the way (taxes, taxes, taxes).

I miss my friends from Zimbabwe. Not very easy to make friends at my age even in a sheltered home.

Nineteen years after leaving Rhodesia I ran into a former schoolmate in San Francisco who brought me up to date on mutual acquaintances including one hacked to death by terrorists with pangas.

It took me 7 years and 3 trips back to Zimbabwe before I became settled and felt Canada was really my home. I still miss certain aspects of the Rhodesian way of life but realize those aspects have changed radically or do not exist anymore.

From a business point of view I came to Canada 10 years too late but I had to fulfill commitments in Rhodesia. It isn't easy to run a business now in Zimbabwe. In Canada there is so much opportunity which I could not take of advantage of due to age. Zimbabwe lost 90% of its wealth creators from 73 onwards which is why post independence progress has been so disappointing. Our children have developed careers which they couldn't have had in Zimbabwe. I was able to found and build another business in Canada at the age of 60.

Have no hope for a happy future here. The attitudes and crime will not go away. If I could leave for Britain I would.

Generally I believe Rhodesians can make it anywhere because of their attitude. Rhodesia will always be "home". My friends and I have to have our annual fix by travelling back to our country. We stay 2-3 weeks every year. Major problem with Rhodesians is having to pay "non-Rhodesian" prices at "our" national parks - always at least 4 times more expensive than for residents- rip off e.g., Zimbabwe ruins $4 for locals US $9 for tourists.

I have been to Australia twice - the only place I've been outside Africa and it's really good to be in a place where only English is spoken and everyone can communicate. That's what I liked most about Rhodesia too.

My quality of life is good but America doesn't feel any way like home. I am still a Rhodie at heart and believe I always will be.

I have accumulated over 50000 sea miles and find it interesting to have met over a dozen ex-Zimbabweans cruising and working as professional sailors.

After leaving Rhodesian/Zimbabwe one should make the best of it and try to obtain what you had (minus servants) and be happy.

A liberation struggle is not over until those who came to liberate have experienced oppression in their own hands. "I have a bird in my hand, so small is it, its life depends on me. Say it is alive and I squash it. Say it is dead and I let it go" but in the end it's up to me if it should live or die depending on my own selfishness."

Initial financial position quite dire but now improved to much the same level it would have been and if Zimbabwe had become a prosperous, stable economy - obviously not the case. Relative strength of sterling means much better off by international comparisons. Do regret loss of Rhodesia but no regrets about leaving Zimbabwe. Life there would be intolerable under current conditions.

I lived in Aberdeen for 4 years and then moved to Glasgow. Been in United Kingdom for 10 years and the first 5 were very unsettled. I always wondered if I would go back to Africa but there were no open doors, especially financially to do so. A Christian minister, who I sought counsel from prayed with me that a "spirit of rest" would come upon me. Within days I found all unsettledness had disappeared and in its place a peace. I have never been unsettled since. God changes people. He is the home of the soul.

Was employed for 25 years by international firm in Rhodesia. In 68 we were offered the choice of staying in the RSA pension fund or joining the Rhodesian fund. I stayed with the RSA fund but my pitiful pension is paid from Zimbabwe because I joined the company in Rhodesia. Something is being concealed. London is making an ex-gratia payment but the total doesn't pay the grocery bill.

We have all had to work extremely hard to achieve what I consider is modest success. It is interesting to note how many ex-Rhodesians have done better than us. I am proud Rhodesians have done so well here. The crime rate worries us tremendously. In Rhodesia the milk money was swiped. In South Africa 2 house burglaries, 2 thefts from garden, 3 cars stolen all when locked and secured, 4 car accidents - all fault of black taxis.

I am proud to be a born Rhodesian but still feel there is an unjustified stigma attached to being a Rhodesian. Cecil John Rhodes was an Englishman and the British were very happy with him with what he did in Africa. It is time for Britain to show a little more honesty and accept that they started the Rhodesias and that they are far more responsible for the welfare of Rhodesians than they seem prepared to accept.

In a management workshop in Johannesburg with middle management of the international company work for we asked how many were from Rhodesia - 12 out of 16 (including the secretary) Not bad infiltration work. We still didn't agree on many issues.

We feel Malawi is a branch of Rhodesia. We have made some wonderful friends - mostly ex-Rhodesians. Our living standard is very similar to home. We have started our own business and have had tremendous support from all. Still get very frustrated at time with the inefficiency as is the case throughout Africa.

My wife and I have had constant employment since leaving Rhodesia and although the early years were a real struggle financially we worked hard and achieved a good standard of living. We consider ourselves fortunate but know that what we have is through our own efforts. We look back on Rhodesia with affection and not a longing for something that we know is no longer there anyway. With so many friends scattered throughout the world it could never be the same. It's a good place for a holiday though!

Built up a major manufacturing company.

Rhodesians who left lose their birthright after some years. I have not yet applied for South Africa citizenship. It is extremely difficult for anyone over 35 years to find employment in SA, even worse now with so called affirmative action, no matter how experienced or qualified you are.

When I came to the USA in 1953 even university professors hadn't heard of Rhodesia. Where are you from? Indonesia? Nobody would then have dreamed what would become of that land. I'm glad I left. Sorry I visited Zimbabwe 5 years ago. Even a 74 visit was better- despite terrorism and the like. I would rather remember it as it was when I was a boy.

We started by cleaning houses, followed by orchard work and foreman in packing shed. Now retired and content.

Finding comparable employment was difficult.

Blessed with good health, I've been lucky. Married for 2nd. time to a younger woman we've survived quite nicely since leaving Rhodesia even though it's taken 5 years to integrate into home country, adjust to COL (with a very low pension) and virtually start over again after 25 years abroad. Having done so, no regrets only fond memories of the Rhodesia we all loved, which bears little resemblance to the Zimbabwe of today. One gets the impression on a recent visit that the bush is closing over the top of it. Pity!

I am very worried about medical facilities to state OAPs. One waits hours at Greys Hospital for only getting one's monthly medicine. To see a doctor is even more difficult. I pray I never really get sick or have an emergency. On the good side my daughter in England has asked me to come and live with them - they have a lovely granny flat. However I am a very proud person and will only go if I have to. My daughter understands my feelings.

When we first arrived wife worked as medical lab techie and worked late shifts - had no transport so relied on public transport. I used to catch bus to town, meet her and both catch bus back (she was afraid of travelling alone at night). Arriving home late one night feeling cold and underprivileged we wrote to Ian Smith asking for some of our money to buy a car. Needless to say the funds never arrived but we did get a very courteous reply. My wife topped New Zealand in her finals exams and I am completing an MBA.

I am constantly amazed at how well Zimbabweans have done outside Africa. I know we had a very good educational system but we have all done very well. Over 90% of my medical school class in Salisbury have left Zimbabwe. Most have specialized and are quite well renowned in their fields. I was always very pleased to see that most ex-Rhodesians did not end up in some Palestinian style refugee camp but went forward in an attempt to better their lives. I have no regrets about being a Rhodesian.

We have been fortunate - we came to this country with nothing except R$1000, some old furniture and a car. After 11 years we were able to retire substantially well off - certainly very much better than had we remained in Rhodesia even had things continued as normal. And yet despite this we have still suffered a loss.

Rhodesians/Zimbabweans seem to beheld in high esteem here. We hoped to own our own home within 5 years and signed on the dotted line after 1 year. Had a planned 4th. child after 3 years. Other 3 children enjoy private education. Have held same job for 5 years and achieved all of above largely on 1 wage. We arrived with some furniture, an old BSA 650 bike -had to sell and $3000. Php 4-19 and Lk 12-31

Very pleased that democracy has come to South Africa without a full scale conflict if the fragile peace can be held for another 2 years the full potential of the region may be realized.

Although I had a hard life in Rhodesia (widowed shortly after my son was born) it was a wonderful life and I wouldn't have missed the experience for anything. I wish that UDI had not been declared and that we had shared government with the Africans - so much loss of life would have been avoided.

I married a wonderful American and lived in Minnesota. The people in mid-West are excellent. After husband died I moved to

California, near family where life and the people are so different. What I dislike most about Zimbabwe is the bribery and corruption, dirty conditions (hotels, border posts etc.). Long queues at banks, post offices, supermarkets etc. and the bad attitude of clerks/ assistants. I cannot ever imagine it improving. My nerves would not stand that life now. I miss the past - terribly!!

I would love to write a book about our experiences in Australia. The years in South Africa were happy and I missed it more than Zimbabwe for a time. I have never settled in Australia although there have been good times and friends here. Financially we find it hard here and plan to go to England where my husband has family. I don't feel I belong anywhere now but incline to England as that is where my roots are and my nature is English.

The reasons we left Zimbabwe have not changed. Our children are doing exceptionally well and have unlimited opportunities for good college education and professionally. Having lived in Zimbabwe for 8 years Rhodesia is dead and gone (we were unable to mention it) and I saw the country change. Zimbabwe is a good place to visit. Politically the whites made a mistake in voting in the RF. If we had gone 15 years to black rule and integrated the blacks we may still have been living there instead of the waste of life etc. in the war.

All members of our family have achieved major successes in work, school and play. Most ex-Rhodesians are too busy building their new lives to worry about Zimbabwe or to get involved in Rhodesian associations. Australia is the natural place for ex-Rhodesians to settle - lifestyle is very similar.

My continuing love and attraction to the old country, sometimes quite emotional is, I suppose, a measure of how good it was. We have a holiday shack/ rented house on the coast with aboriginal neighbours(unemployed). We work hard on the house, painting the roof etc. while they sit in their back yard getting drunk on our taxes - a notable turnaround. That aspect doesn't bother me too much - just means you have less leisure time!

I recently spent a month in Zimbabwe. My main observation was that the government continues to find more ways to steal money from the people so they can continue to get fatter while the masses continue to get worse off. The whites still seem to enjoy a similar life style to before although the economic conditions along with the drought make farming much more difficult than before. Also there is almost no more white middle class.

On arriving at a rural Vermont school - the only one prepared to employ me based on my credentials and without an interview the school board were surprised to learn Africans were both black and white. I write this from the only home we ever owned in a town of 2000. From a family of 5 on arrival we are now 11. As grandson of an 1890 pioneer I am aware of the conditions he faced. Nevertheless the challenges of pioneering in a new land today are still formidable. I am doubly blessed in my Rhodesian heritage and my home.

Coming to South Africa was right for career. Strange times indeed. I managed to see the world from South Africa. I need to see this change in. However I know that being married to a Pom we could agree to move at any time. So be it. We remain in a state of flux. Does the packing ever stop?

When I left Rhodesia I joined the international staff of major firm and was promoted to MD Botswana and then Zambia. In Botswana was appointed to presidential commission on Land tenure (most interesting). In Zambia faced many problems. In both territories achieved significant growth in market share.

I found it extremely difficult to adjust to life here in United Kingdom with periods of depression over 4-5 years. Now have more settled outlook but still regret leaving.

The greatest problem has been bought about by the devaluation of the Z$ and the reluctance of the British government to assist British expatriates in this regard notwithstanding the fact that the vast majority of British immigrants to Rhodesia in the 1945-50 era served their country well in WW2. I did for 6½ years.

I am lucky enough at the moment to spend 6 months in Scotland and 6 months in Zimbabwe and South Africa.

I long for Africa and its climate and my wife loves England. In South Africa I was first occupied with RCG and then returned to parish ministry. In England I am technically retired but in practice and busy with church work. I regret Rhodesia very much but have no time for regrets.

Arabic taxi driver laughed his head off because we said we came from Africa but thinks we are joking because we are not black!

Since arriving in the United Kingdom I have qualified as a solicitor and am a partner in a middle sized firm of solicitors in private practice.

We visit South Africa each year on holiday. This holiday could easily be in Zimbabwe except I refuse to visit a country that charges tourists more than the locals.

Transferred to Federation in 59 by multi-national employer and was Salisbury branch manager until retirement in Oct 79. Having my own house I was happy to stay in Zimbabwe and gave my services freely to WVS after retirement. However, was offered accommodation on South Coast and emigrated. This was a disaster. After 10 years in South Africa I returned to my native United Kingdom a year ago.

Lost too many friends in the war in Rhodesia and never wanted to return for that reason. It would be too emotional for me to handle. My sister is a financial prisoner in SA, having lost all in Zimbabwe, she cannot face the same loss in leaving South Africa so lives once again under the chaos of black rule. Such a waste of lives and all to achieve.....absolutely nothing.

Rhodesians have done very well in UK. From my year at Peterhouse Richard Astaire? is CEO of Dalgety PLC, Neville Bush? is CEO of Blenheim PLC and Rupert Pennant-Rea was deputy governor of the Bank of England until recently. Many other Rhodesians I know are in senior positions.

After losing everything in Rhodesia and starting again we discovered the only thing worthy of our complete trust and faith was the Lord Jesus Christ. Putting our hopes etc. into man made wealth, only to see it vanish overnight led us, and many other Rhodesians, to seek a meaning in life that no man can take away. 52-60 Southern Rhodesia, 60-68 Zambia, 68-76 Rhodesia, 76-86 South Africa.

Proud to have been a Rhodesian but cannot live in past. Don't deliberately try to forget- one cannot blot out nearly 3 happy decades but life moves on. Families move away and one has a living to make. Although Rhodesians and South Africans constitute main segment of our circle this is not deliberate.

As our pension comes from Zimbabwe we begrudge the fact that the Z$ is only a tenth of what it was due to the mismanagement of the government.

Since 1927 - so many memories, so many friends gone. Too full - too sad. Perfidious Albion!

Won 6 motor cycle road racing championships for Rhodesia. Awarded MBE for services to sport

I brought my Datsun 120Y with me in 81. I had UK number plates but left them in the boot as I thought other motorists would be less annoyed by my dithering when finding my way in strange places. Several people asked if I was from Russia - RSR meant that to them. After 6 months police caught me for different number plates to licence. After much correspondence and visit from local bobby I was forgiven. He was very interested in my Rhodie Datsun as it was so different to his. Bonnet air vents interested him most.

Am at top of my new career - managing a large national trust property. Took me 6 months to find a job. My first regular job was managing a large poultry farm. Then moved to Northern Ireland to manage a lovely National Trust house. We are much nearer our aging parents. We cannot live the quality of life that we did in Zimbabwe - we love Zimbabwe.

My wife and I came to the United Kingdom initially for me to undertake further training. After 5 years here we tried to get back to Rhodesia but found the doors were closed to us so we had to stay on here. We had 5 children by this time which meant we couldn't afford return tickets for all of us.

I returned to United Kingdom because of severe ill-health. Difficulties were not knowing where to live, little funds, no understanding of social security system, no close friends. A son aged 25 who could not/ did not know how to help/ did not understand a desperately sick mother with arthritis and lupus since 1959 and many related problems from stress and having to work to keep 2 sons in school to A level. Husband had flown the nest, no support from him at all. Emigrating to United Kingdom after 27 years like emigrating to a foreign country.

Left Rhodesia in 77 with very heavy heart. Moved to Durban for 3 years then to United Kingdom for sons to get UK citizenship. Returned to South Africa and remained there. Unable to get employment and returned to United Kingdom when we saw South Africa heading for black rule too. But heart still in Africa.

Became Rhodesian citizens. Two Rhodesian born grandchildren. Travelled extensively throughout Rhodesia over the years. Wife feels her great hero is Ian Smith and second only to Winston Churchill.

I have a more senior position in London than I had in Rhodesia. When I began house hunting I told the agent I was looking for 4 bed detached house on half or quarter acre and that I was prepared to pay up to £10000. He nearly had hysterics and I began to learn the facts of life very quickly after that.

With my working career in its twilight I wonder if I can settle in the United Kingdom mainly due to weather. Will stay working overseas as long as possible but mainly for financial rewards.

My belief is that Rhodesia was defeated from within and not by external forces. We should all have held on and preserved what we had built up.

We both were disillusioned with British public as compared to Rhodesian/ Zimbabwe public of all races. Previously one could excuse a drop in standards with "Shame, yena muntu khupella". Now the general standards are considerably lower and that excuse no longer applies. One feels that having unusually high standards ourselves we shamefully underestimated the very high standards to be found generally among Rhodesian/Zimbabwe Africans.

My Rhodesian born son was murdered in Johannesburg in 1990. My other son wrote a book "Choosing your next boss" which is on Compuserve and Internet.

I am most fortunate that I work full time for a South African company but with a dwindling Zimbabwe pension life will become harder when I finally retire at 70 next year.

Left Zimbabwe for political reasons and for kids security. Went to South Africa for same reasons and also left for son's future (I disagreed with national service in SA) only to arrive in United Kingdom and have son join Royal Marines - you just can't win.

The fact I decided to move to England to seek employment (leaving my wife and 2 children in SA) with plans to bring them to the United Kingdom eventually has contributed to the break up of my marriage.

As a female I reached the top of the tree in my profession of accountancy. I would not have been able to do this if I had stayed in the UK. During my years in Rhodesia my family and I had a most enjoyable time and we also worked very hard. But things changed very much in Zimbabwe with everything becoming political. We still had to work hard but things became different and there was no longer the happiness and laughter that was about before.

When I first arrived in United Kingdom life was new and enjoyable. I had been to the United Kingdom many times on holiday but living here is quite different. After the newness wore off life was not easy and I seemed to be short of money most of the time even though I was helped by my parents still in Africa. I met a lady and her adult daughter getting off a bus in Newcastle. They were on their way to Scotland but I had known them both in Wankie where I was born. They now live in South Africa and I have never seen them again.

Since retiring in 89 in Zimbabwe I have achieved very little. I live on a pension which gets smaller as the years go by due to exchange rates. However I know many also from Zimbabwe who are living on smaller pensions. Nevertheless we enjoyed our lives in Rhodesia/Zimbabwe - we lived there for 32 years.

I feel very different to my friends and work associates about most issues. Because of my experiences I feel stronger and more equipped to deal with life in general. My attitude and outlook is very positive feeling I can take anything thrown at me. This is because of the great adversity I have had from losing the country and way of life I truly loved and cared with great pride.

Very curious about your agenda behind these questions, considering its limited appeal at large and necessary current irrelevance to all but a tiny minority scattered worldwide of nostalgics.

To have been born and raised in Rhodesia was a gift beyond price and that left me with a lot of happy memories. I still get the urge to smell the dust, climb on a granite boulder and admire a msasa or mopane tree. But I have no regrets about leaving Rhodesia - for the place is no more and we are very happy here and gradually getting used to Americans. And where else could I reach the peak of my specialty in science?

If we were able to obtain the right to our residence by birthright we would return.

I work at a timeshare resort and it is rather amusing to find that I am accepted more readily by the black staff members and the guests who end up by treating me as one of the family. Most of these guests are rather upset if I happen to be on days off or leave during their stay.

I basically have not benefited from the move but my wife and children definitely have. All the children are better off now than if we had remained in Zimbabwe but for my part there is hardly a day goes by when I don't think of the country that was my home for 3 decades and of which I shall always be extremely proud to say I was a part of Rhodesia.

Generally speaking our move to South Africa with our three children has proved successful.

MD and Chairman of 4 companies in group of 80. Listed on JSE. Left after take -over. Now sole owners of company -

turnover R800000. Have found some ex-Rhodesians have become professional con artists.

Since leaving Rhodesia with R30000 pension payout I have bought and sold 5 houses by going better each time and this is house 6. I had a shell built and did all the interior woodwork myself to good old fashioned standards.

If a Rhodesian is deported to which country must they go? So why are Rhodesians not allowed back to their country of birth. Why must a Rhodesian pay for a visa if their record is clean. I left Zimbabwe because my husband died there and I could not manage alone with rising costs of lights, water and rates.

In their achievements, their mores, their wholesomeness I believe the Rhodesian people to have been unique. Rhodesia was the coming together of several cultures guided by the very best of the British background. One good outcome of Zimbabwe is that the countries where Rhodesians have settled will all be enriched by the influx of Rhodesian standards and people.

Daughter has achieved very well as personnel manager and acting general manager. This for a young female in South Africa is an outstanding achievement. Wife wrote book on terrorist war in association with 2 others, published in Pretoria.

Our children were brought up and went to school in the best environment ever.

Sad lack of trustworthiness and prevailing tendency to measure a man's worth by his material possessions. Corrupt business practices and the astonishing arrogance and aggressive attitude of wives of successful business men. Intolerable level of crime. I can no longer move from A to B without the threat of being robbed, mugged, hijacked and murdered. I can no longer on holiday with any peace of mind that my home will not be broken into, my possessions stolen and every room trashed.

Husband, Zambian by birth, Rhodesian by heart now has his own business. He was transferred to Lourenco Marques 68-74 and we loved the place. I believe the major adaptation we had to make there made it easier to leave Rhodesia in 79 as well as the confrontation we were forced to have with Mozambique when it went black. Husband sent his money from Mozambique to South Africa not Rhodesia which made it easier to leave in 79.

Filed Reservist BSAP. Twice blown up by land mine - hearing impaired. Sons served in Rhodesia Regiment.

I am one of a number of ex-Zimbabweans living in a small town in the eastern Cape interior. Almost all have located there because of low property prices - none of us could afford to retire to the cost or live in a major town. Many are struggling to make ends meet especially those on Rhodesian pensions.

I was gainfully employed in my profession on my return to South Africa and despite being widowed 15 years ago I have retained my equilibrium and live a successful and peaceful life with the love and support of my two sons - one in South Africa and the other in Australia.

I was forced to apply for a South African passport because the Zimbabwe authorities refused to renew my Zimbabwe passport.

People in South Africa are definitely not as friendly as Rhodies - don't pop in for cup or a chat. Pace of life in South Africa much faster than Rhodesia BUT workers, black in particular not a patch on Rhodesian Matabeles - closest are Zulus in Natal, others seem too tired to work.

I often think we should have stayed on in Zimbabwe instead of scattering far and wide. People seem happy and still have a good way of life in Zimbabwe although they live behind locked and gated walls. The Africans one meets are generally friendly behind counters at petrol stations etc. But one knows crime is rife so take necessary steps. South Africa - time will tell.

Rhodesia had a civil service and police force second to none. I am very proud to have been associated with both disciplines.

Our first job was with tyre company in OFS. Arrived in May with R185. The weather was freezing and we had no money for winter clothes. We kitted my husband out and I stayed warm under the duvet. It was the coldest winter we had in 50 years. I return regularly - the call of home is great. There have been many changes and when I get to church I am welcomed back with open arms - they always ask when are you coming back - that's by all races. My husband died after 3 years and I had difficulty settling in a boxed in bungalow after the rural life.

Alas Rhodesia has gone. We were swimming upstream. Now I see the end was inevitable. At the time UDI seemed right but it is an insane world with a huge white guilt complex - we were sacrificed to incompetence but it could be no other way.

Husband was tobacco grower in Darwin area and before that in Rhodesian Army. He could not settle and returned to Zimbabwe in 87 to farm tobacco in Headlands. Had the worst drought in living memory and had to return to South Africa having sold electrical equipment to pay expenses. Bought a farm in Mooiplaas, E. Cape. We left this in 93 because of the security situation and put in tenants. The homestead was demolished by blacks in Sept/Oct 94. There is nothing left other than a few bricks. Insurance didn't pay and worry killed husband in December 94.

Retrenched in Jan 95 - now self employed in wholesale distribution. Intend emigrating to Australia in 3 years as retired person - sponsored by son. I was resident in Northern and Southern Rhodesia at time of independence - now experiencing third demise of country of adoption and relegation to second class citizenship.

Having recently gone through change to black government in South Africa you realize we all left Rhodesia too quickly and had we all stayed our live would not have changed that much. No matter how long you've been out of the country when you drive back over the Limpopo you are still going “home”.

From arrival till 85 we lived well. Went to US and Canada for 7 week holiday and bought new car. but since then the country has deteriorated and the farm we were on was sold. Since we have been on a downward slide. I have been unemployed for 2 years and have now started a small grocery shop in one of the black reserves. We manage but only just. What a far cry from good old Rhodesia and all the dreams and aspirations we had.

When I arrived at Tokyo Baptist Church my first baptism was of Zimbabweans from the embassy.

Easy in hindsight we should have gradually handed over to majority rule. It would now be a shining example to Africa of how much potential and innovative the integration process could have been.

Authored 5 books.

My big problem is the devaluation of the Zimbabwe currency greatly reducing my pension.

As with many Rhodesians (not Zimbabweans) I very much miss the Rhodesia we knew during the war - the spirit, the friendship, the sharing by all and even the war which gave us all such a joint purpose and gave meaning to being a "Rhodie."

I left Rhodesia just before my teenage years, finished my education as a registered nurse. Travelled through England, Europe, Australia. Now married with 19 month son and a second due in 2 months. I found the first few years hard, having to adapt but now I love New Zealand, my kiwi husband and family. I feel the best way one can cope with a major upheaval such as Rhodesians had to deal with is a positive attitude, don't dwell on the past, be glad of you happy memories and get on with the future. Time does NOT stand still.

All over the world I have bumped into and often befriended Africans from other countries. I am beginning to realize that African governments have failed their brightest and their best as well as their middle classes. Those who have choices have made them and voted with their feet. But to the last person they love their country and the continent and would consider returning if they trusted the economy, politics and the law. In other words Rhodesians are a special but not unique migration.

We used to belong to RW but now live some distance from centres and activities. Rhodesians migrating to South Africa may have jumped from the frying pan into the fire as the present government is all pro third (rate) world to the detriment of the white minority. There is a lowering of all vital standards due to the inexperienced administration.

My heart is still in Rhodesia. Social politics leave me unmoved. I just can't feel passionately about South Africa as I did about Rhodesia. In a lot of ways I still feel alien.

We found employment impossible as no one wanted to pay a 60 year old a living wage. For 5 years we house sat. Made masses of friends, enjoyed being nomads and accumulated enough money to buy a house. Still have friends and house but have lost my husband. The only thing making life difficult now is the erosion of the Z$ and still deteriorating security in South Africa. On the whole life is good and I enjoy a yearly visit to Zimbabwe.

As a family we were very comfortable and a little complacent in Rhodesia. This move has definitely made us more adventurous and motivated the survival instinct in us, resulting in achieving a higher standard of living and career success. Emigration was very difficult at the time but we have definitely benefited in the long term.

Have a very good stud cattle herd, plenty of problems as you all know. Lots of ex-Rhodesians here in Pietersburg. Miss my old farming days in Rhodesia.

Grandfather was pioneer belonging to BSA Co. Police which escorted the Pioneer column to Rhodesia in 1890. It is my very great regret that I had to leave this heritage behind. Four generations of this family fought in the Rhodesian services i.e. occupation of Rhodesia, WW1, WW2 and Rhodesian bush war. I was the first resident in Que Que to have his name inscribed in the book of civic honours in Que Que in 1966 for services rendered to Que Que.

I still yearn terribly for the wonderful life I had in Rhodesia and reminisce every morning on my way to the office. Would love to retire there one day and am seriously contemplating it.

We live in the new South Africa to be near our children who left Rhodesia as did many other young married people.

I have 4 very Rhodesian children who still yearn for "home". We are all considering going "home". South Africa has been very good to us but our bond with our people is very strong. We seek each other out at every opportunity. I am customer services manager for a large store in Johannesburg. I lived in Pietersburg for 10 years where many businesses are managed by Rhodesians - we are everywhere in good positions.

Six months after arrival in South Africa husband had severe stroke and had to retire at age 56 being unable to work. After a few years we had no funds and had to join long queues at state hospitals. Fortunately husband came into inheritance so we were able to buy a town house but because of inflation we have to watch every penny and lead a very quiet life.

I was born in South Africa but consider myself a Rhodesian although I again live in South Africa.

One still tends to find Rhodesians are more reliable friends than South Africans and easier to mix with. From the employment side they are still far superior to the locals. The older one gets the more you appreciate the life we had there and if things were different it would be the only country to be in.

This is a great project. My fear however is that the large body of Rhodesians not in associations will be missed and thus render the statistics invalid.

When I first saw RW I thought its logo of "speaking the same language" almost fatuous. However having wandered round Europe and Africa since then I have seen the transformation/ animation of people when they get together as "Rhodesians" especially those getting on in years (I'm still young). Rhodesia still exists and people do speak the same language. Here Rhodies are becoming "consultants" on political matters rather than "whenwes".

Retired from PTC as a chief technician and joined Telkom South Africa. Retired in 93 as chief technical officer. Wife was secretary/book-keeper to local council and resigned to move to South Africa and was employed as computer book-keeper until ill-health forced retirement.

In 48 Nats came to power in South Africa. The destruction of my culture began immediately. I emigrated to Northern Rhodesia. In 64 I lost my adopted country. I moved to Rhodesia and again lost my adopted country in 1980. In 89 while not being an admirer of South Africa I opted for it on a Hobson's choice basis. Three months after my arrival we were notified of majority rule - tough. No cultural majority or minority can fairly rule over another. I'll survive but sometimes I wonder what for. Money and survival have limitations.

While I was very upset at having to leave Rhodesia for personal reasons I have no regrets nor do any other family members as we have all done better in our respective economic lives than we would have achieved in Rhodesia - despite me being a divisional head in the then Rhodesia Railways.

We shall probably emigrate to New Zealand in 96 but it will be with great reluctance. The level of violence, rising costs (tax included) and the current affirmative action program are making us uncomfortable.

I made a study of Rhodesian culture. In essence it is a sub culture of British (English, Irish, Scots, Welsh) with strong South African (Afrikaner) influence. It is rooted in the pre UDI era but amalgamated into a unique blend after UDI. It is largely characterized by values and survives in Zimbabwe to this day.

I hope my children and grandchildren in South Africa and Zimbabwe will enjoy a fruitful and secure life. The future still contains many imponderables for both countries.

When one day I die then I shall return to Zimbabwe. All arrangements been paid. In 65 I bought grave next to my late husband. Rhodesia/Zimbabwe is still No. 1 by me. I had a feeling as if I was born there. My eldest son still lives there with family.

I do not in any way regret my 30 years in Rhodesia and had made arrangements to leave Rhodesia nearly 12 months before UDI. This had no influence on my decision to go to the UK. My daughter and grand daughter have all visited Zimbabwe and love the country as do my South African descendants.

In my circumstances I just had to dig my heels in and find work, accommodation, schooling for my daughter. But we have worked hard and achieved our goals. Still divorced but not prepared to move again. The change was just too much and too rapid. If I hadn't got divorced would still be in good old Rhodesia. Came out with R1300, no electrical items or furniture but managed.

Rhodesia taught me not to complain but to calmly look at the problem and then solve it to the best of my ability. Here all the Rhodesians I know have done just that. Our pensions have halved but we have anticipated this and taken necessary action to survive. We cannot and do not complain.

So grateful to have had those wonderful years in Rhodesia 47-70. Even widowed years 70-81 were happy and productive. Still happy and productive in RSA.

Until about 2 years ago I used to have nightmares about the war in Rhodesia. I would scream, shout and beat my husband. I was a child when it started and I never want my children to grow up being woken and led to hide in dens for the night. I have since taught myself and now my children not to be frightened of the dark. I'm slightly deaf from having to use an FN rifle.

The happiest days of my life were spent in Rhodesia. The funniest thing is that my best friends all left years after us and we have all ended up in Kent. RW is a great organization and I hope it expands. One funny thing - after knowing my neighbours 2 doors away casually for several years I found out they were in Bulawayo at the same time as myself.

Having supported the RF government since (1960) I feel they should have allowed me to take out more than Z$1000 when I emigrated. The amount should have been related to the number of years of residence, especially as the $ has been devalued to present levels. However Australia has been good to me and I am now (after a lot of hard work) in a better financial position than I was in Rhodesia

Both employed at ages 53 and 62 when 3 million unemployed. Major problems overcoming depression and stress from having lost everything we possessed when leaving Zimbabwe.

I took army experience as an opportunity to learn from rather than an obligation to be resented. It left me with a clear view that I was unsuited to indoor paperwork hence I now have an active job in drilling for oil off shore. Number of connections I make with people through contacts I made in the army still astounds me.

At age 67 I was widowed after 48 years and had to find a job. Everywhere I applied I was told I was too old. The last agency run by an ex-Rhodesian suggested I get a copy of The Lady magazine and try for a job as companion or housekeeper. Took her advice and was fortunate to come on a weeks trial as a care giver to a disabled lady. Six years later I am still here and treated as one of a wonderful family and now feel I have 2 wonderful families.

SA has been good to me. I represented South Africa in highboard diving v. USA in a test match in 88. I represented Transvaal for 5 years as a Springbok diver (88-92). Was Transvaal and north Transvaal highboard champ (88-92). Represented east Transvaal at trampoline. Got an LLM from RAU. Admitted as professional town clerk. Son was first South African to represent South Africa in sport in Moscow in trampoline and daughter represented South Africa in trampoline and Transvaal in diving.

Devaluation of Z$ makes us battle to make ends meet.

We don't look for Rhodesians but often seem to come across them socially. We went on a luncheon trip out of Sydney harbour and discovered 5 Rhodesians on board including the chef.

I only left Zimbabwe because of high unemployment. My army career became impossible due to the "stay behind and fuck it up" behavior of some senior white officers.

Wonderful to see Zimbabwe at last visit and relative lack of exchange control.

The saddest thing about this survey is the reason for its genesis. There is no earthly reason why emigrants from Rhodesia/ Zimbabwe should congregate together, merely because of their origins and invariably become a coterie of whining whenwes. Better far to adapt to new conditions, retain good memories but do not use them to excuse failure to make a new life.

I was able to capitalize on the building boom of the 80s. My wife and I worked and also renovated a number of houses that we bought and lived in while we did them up and then sold. Within a year we were on the first step up the ladder and within ten we are comfortably off by average standards and if we were to convert sterling to Z$ then we would be millionaires. Not a bad thought!

Have a mortgage, wife and child. Work all the hours God gives. Have a job but still can't make ends meet. Would love to be out of financial difficulty.

Sole achievement - survival in an environment where apart from a few friends I feel I do not belong. On a local train a fellow passenger was an African with a mountain of luggage. Arriving at Newcastle he looked bewildered. On impulse I greeted him "Mangwanani" and asked which platform he wanted. I received an amazed but hearty response plus tribal handshake. He was going to Halifax for 2 weeks training before returning to Hartley. "And you Madam when will you go home?" I had to say I would not go back. "That is a shame. I have been here 3 weeks and would not like to live here. There is no sunshine. Everybody needs sunshine." My feelings exactly! I found a helpful BR man who brought a suitable trolley for all the luggage and the two departed for the Halifax train. Amazing how just the bare minimum of another language can establish rapport.

If finance were not a problem my wife and I would in all probability emigrate to South Africa.

Author of several books in the financial services and corporate sectors. Generally my family has settled in well. I have had ups and downs in business and got into serious financial trouble in the recession. Taking a long time to recover from that.

The Rhodesian educational system equipped us very well for survival and life in different cultures. Australians know little of Southern Africa and appear very insular and parochial. We survived retrenchment 15 months after arrival and moved interstate 3 times in 10 year to stay employed. Two children have entered university and 3rd. started high school. Middle child got very high TEE results in WA and fell just outside top 100 students in state in 94 when 18 months younger than classmates.

Miss the countryside, animals and open nature of Rhodesians and knowing nearly everyone you met in town. Really miss the weather.

We have carved out a good life for ourselves in Australia. Our children have all achieved well in their chosen fields and we have 2 children at Australian Defence Forces Academy where our daughter is the cadet captain with over 900 cadets under her. We have come to love it here and would not want to live anywhere else - not even Zimbabwe.

We moved from both Rhodesia and South Africa for the security of our kids hoping they would not move too far away when older. While health, security and education are OK we are worse off for leaving while the kids are better off. So we achieved what we set out to do but have lost "fame and fortune" ourselves which is not easy to live with.

Children born in Kenya. Moved to Rhodesia where they were educated (very well). Moved to South Africa which took us in when Australia wouldn't (for which we are grateful). When permission finally came we took it up.

I re-qualified at Wits in 82-84 in 13 subjects of the LL.B that I had already passed at UR. Then came to Australia and had to re qualify here. Now on final leg of opening own practice. Its been a long haul since I left Zimbabwe in 82. One of the cases I had to study in Wits in 82 was a case in which I appeared as defence counsel in Rhodesia in 70s. I was able to tell the class and the lecturer it was my case they were training on.

Will never forget my upbringing in Rhodesia and have many memories but now call Australia home and am proud to be Australian. Being in Customs and Excise for 6 years I should have known trying to smuggle cigarettes into United Kingdom was a misdemeanor - a fine and duty claimed half of my precious holiday allowance on arrival and I was left with £75 and a suit-case to start a new life.

Our slightly retarded daughter gave us incentive to leave Zimbab-we. If we had grown up children we would have stayed. Thinking seriously of spending 6 months in Australia and 6 in Zimbabwe on retirement. Neither has really settled in Australia although we tried hard to relocate. All ex Rhodies we met have done well - that must indicate something in the Rhodesian character.

Most Australians mistake us for South Africans (racist) or Eng-lish (pommie bastard). However once you set them right (if you get a chance) they are a bit more relaxed - either they consider we have better traits than both or more likely they are plain ignorant. Australia is a continent with one nation and they seem to think Africa is the same.

Travelled round Australia when "Rhodesian" pension was still worth something. Later when Z$ was losing value had to settle down and live life of lower class Australian - still better than a devalued "Zimbabwean". Sale of my vintage car paid for our house so we live comfortably but we can't afford extravagance.

Widowed 2 years after arrival in Australia. As we had become citizens I got widows pension and benefits long before I had been here 10 years. As the Z$ devalued this was a great relief. I can afford private health cover which has been of great benefit to me as my health has been a problem.

Adding to my present qualifications after 3 years part-time study, much of it in Afrikaans, becoming partially bilingual. Tragic murder of my first wife. Meeting and marrying a Rhodesian girl. Two lovely sons. Successful emigration of brother and sister to Brisbane.

We would never have left Rhodesia but for the change in government. Husband died 6 months after arrival. Life was very difficult for several years. Children have done extremely well. I have a qualified pharmacist, first officer with Quantas and a professional musician. I remarried an Anglican minister and we are happy. I thank God for all my blessings and that I had so many wonderful years in Rhodesia which was without doubt the best country in the world.

Just had another short but wonderful holiday to Zimbabwe. I ask myself: Do we exist and they live? As we drudge through the day to day hassles of paying off big mortgage, keeping house and garden sans servants, never dropping in spontaneously on friends often I wonder if we did the right thing. But it doesn't take long to realize that life in Australia is the real thing. The life in Zimbabwe is unrealistic, transparent and probably short lived but wonderful while it lasts. Perhaps 6 months a year in each country!

We have done very much better than we had hoped. We paid off our house in 9 years and spent another $30000 in making it comfortable. Now that I am an Australian pensioner we are very well looked after in our daily lives.

Our main problem was settling in Sydney's vast urban sprawl after Harare. We knew very few ex-Rhodesians to discuss how we felt (leaving our home, different work environment, education, weather, finance etc.) It's always a pleasure to meet ex

Rhodesians/Zimbabweans and feel at ease in their company not having to think before speaking.

We both work. Have not been unemployed. Have made wonderful new friends. We built our own home and look forward to raising our 3 Australian born children in a safe and loving home. Still have Rhodesian friends.

We found a major camping difference - the night is dead silent as compared to the animal/insect noises of the nights of Africa.

Have always managed to own own house and find work. Find reasonably compatible people to play tennis and bridge with. Now receive UK old age, UK national health, Australian veterans and Rhodesian/Zimbabwe civil service pensions. Is this a record?

The stringent financial rules would have made our resettlement from Rhodesia impossible if we hadn't made previous investments in UK, Australia, and South Africa and had relatives here who provided accommodation until we rearranged our finances. Our sympathies are with our friends we left behind and are aware of the COL in Zimbabwe and the rate of Z$6.25 to $1 Australian.

Unemployment is an on-going problem among ex-Rhodesians with the threat of redundancy never far away. Probably more than half who have migrated are under-employed in some cases, holding managerial positions back there and now labouring.

Rhodesia had a great easy-going life style, but in the war/ sanctions fostered a great sense of community and patriotism. Unfortunately it also led to a Marxist take over and I felt I had to leave. I would love to go back but I doubt if the country will ever recover and be as prosperous as it once was.

We now think of ourselves as Australian. We spent 12 days in Zimbabwe in 93 mainly meeting old friends. On the whole we found Harare depressing - dirty and crime ridden. You need a good income to enjoy the facilities still available but its tough living on a government pension.

I strongly resent being referred to as an ex-Rhodesian. One doesn't encounter ex-Greeks, ex-Canadians or ex-Australians when these people relocate. I am a Rhodesian or Zimbabwean Australian.

It was a great privilege to be employed by Conex and provided a wonderful base for my career to date.

At our age we consider the fact that we managed to pay for a house here in South Africa to be a marvelous achievement and are grateful that in our 70's my wife and I are comfortably settled near our children who emigrated in 1980.

South Africa was a difficult country to settle in but afforded me time to gain experience for the USA which is easier to live in and offers unlimited possibilities for anyone prepared to work hard.

Both my wife and I miss Rhodesia but do not regret leaving Zimbabwe. Although we joined RASA we have tried not to be labeled "whenwes" but have made few South African friends other than those with Rhodesian connections.

My main problem is loneliness since my husband died in 89. There are very few Rhodesians from better days here who were our friends in Bulawayo. I would dearly love to return to Natal to be near some of them but my meager widow's pension will not allow me to move back. I find South Africans only want to know you for what you can give or do for it even if you are against the project concerned.

Thoroughly enjoy RW. Super to get news of former pupils and friends from mining days (Arcturus mine) also many other facets of Rhodesian life.

As a family we have settled well, we believe due to Rhodesian upbringing and living standards. I have been successful through hard work and made a major success of my career. I am retired but continue to work as consultant in sub-Saharan Africa.

While lucky enough to be in a pensionable occupation and daily waiting "the chop" (with free accommodation) one still struggles to keep some semblance of normality. I cannot agree with an oft heard opinion "Rhodesians were spoilt". Rhodesians of my acquaintance worked hard, played hard and did not deserve to be treated as they were.

Had we known South Africa was going the way it has we would probably, no undoubtedly, had a re-think on emigration and where to - we weren't in the employable bracket so it was a case of doing the best we could on what we had - Zimbabwe pensions are pitiful. How some survive beats me as they get far less than me and we get peanuts.

South Africa has been good to us but we are proud to say we have been good to South Africa. However we still miss Rhodesia and the wonderful life we had there

Since arriving in Canada I have joined the reserves and am now a captain.

I am not a racialist but do feel the world would be a better place if left in the hands of civilized people.

It is a pity the British government decided that Rhodesia must go black - they sold us down the river! The politicians of Britain were totally dishonest - using double standards and Sir Roy Welensky at the break up of the Federation had not the brains to see what was happening. The breaking of Rhodesia should never have happened. We were multi racial. South Africa is only now where we were at the start of UDI. South Africa will one day be worse than Zimbabwe.

Am always welcomed on my visits to Zimbabwe and never made to feel alien. Zimbabwe people are very courteous in all departments

Very hard for Zimbabweans to assimilate into society as most refer to us as "whenwes". As a result most of us tend not to mix with locals and this also creates a problem. Hopefully now the situation will rectify itself.

CEO and majority shareholder of business I left Rhodesia to run. Major shareholder in 3 other successful business ventures.

I spontaneously warm towards any members of the "last white tribe" I meet (even the "green" ones) and I am happy to say I find 9 out of 10 of them respond the same way

Chairman of RASA Pretoria, RASA National executive member. Run the only photo interpretation lab in SA, mapping by computer off aerial photos - I never even saw a computer till 85. We never had electricity on our farm so South Africa was a cultural shock.

When I arrived in South Africa aged 50 I studied at UCT and achieved a B.Music degree.

Husband born Umtali 1910, son of 1894 pioneer and was a true Rhodesian. As he was 68 and I, 60 when we came to South Africa we could not work but we managed. My widow's pension from Zimbabwe is about R500 p.m. Fortunately I have a few investments else I would be in sore straits.

I remember as a child how dangerous it was just going to town, school -doing necessary things. Community fantastic. If my dad was on camp other couples would check on our welfare continuously

Rhodesia was a wonderful place in the "old days". The country is still a beautiful holiday destination but the poverty among the black people makes me very sad. They thought an election would improve their future but they are worse off now. I hope their future brightens and South Africa doesn't have the same fate. I believe white Rhodesians had more concern then than Mugabe's government now (much more!).

We are residents of Home Trust in a lovely environment with transport facilities at minimal rates. Residents are friendly and sociable with a fair number of Rhodies, which makes it pleasant.

Whenever one talks to people in banks, supermarkets, sports days, school functions they are always Rhodesians (friendly hardworking types). South Africans do not like to speak to strangers in queues. Still trying to work out why the Boer war has not yet been forgotten.

When I left Zimbabwe I was a town person - could not stand farming or cattle etc. Now I have completely changed and am hooked on farm life.

Husband was railway employee and became very discouraged when the blacks took over and he had inexperienced men put in positions over him. We came to Joburg where he had a good job with accommodation supplied. He had a very hard physical job and after 2 year here he died. It has been a difficult 8 years for me but the Lord has been my strength and provider.

Since 89 I have visited Zimbabwe as often as possible and now do so once a year. I have noted considerable improvements in past 3 years as one can now get almost anything provided it is possible to pay - vehicles, spare parts. It is noticeable how happy and affluent the minority is and how miserable and worried the masses are - worried about where the next meal is coming from or the next job - the once happy friendly smiles are not so evident these days.

Absence of childhood and long term friends, sense of not fully belonging in either USA or Zimbabwe, being a smaller fish in a bigger pond.

The trauma of retiring as well as emigrating was most profound.

I was born in Bulawayo of Pioneer stock from both sides of my family. Educated at PE and lived in northern Rhodesia where I married an Irish lass and we had 4 children - one of whom still lives in Salisbury. Very proud of Rhodesia but the opposite of Zimbabwe.

Progress in both financial and employment situation - establishing 2 part time businesses - photography and a machine facility for steel.

A a pilot/world traveller I firmly believe Rhodesians were the best on earth. We gave the new Zimbabwe a try for 8 years but the "bully boy" politicians forced us out of a superb job and paid up home. We could return to settle because the present lunatic, arrogant, ignorant government will not change in my life time. Work permit problems are guaranteed. Salaries do not match ridiculous bond repayments.

Have only fond memories of how people pulled together, helped each other during the difficult times of petrol rationing. Recall myself and 2 other company directors cycling to work to set example to our staff - only to be passed by an employee on a putt-putt with a helmet on "large man on small bike."

We're glad we came for one really good reason. We appreciate what we had in Rhodesia and don't take it for granted anymore. We see things there in a new perspective.

My wife's grandfather, Gifford, led the Edenburg Trek from Edenburg, South Africa to Chipinga and was granted land there by Cecil Rhodes.

My youngest son and I have from nothing (i.e. trailer load of possessions towed by a Citroen Club) built an engineering business with assets of R200,000. My youngest son and I are partners in this concern and employ 3 bodies - 2 South Africans and 1 Rhodesian.

My children have done very well - Professional chemist - Ph.D., daughter is B.Mus (1st. class), LSRM, UNISA LM, RULM and second son M.Sc. Eng (Agrica)

We are in the process of emigrating to New Zealand as we see no future for our children in South Africa.

Two years after immigrating to the BSAP in Southern Rhodesia from Scotland I took out citizenship and change my British passport to a Southern Rhodesian one because I loved the country so much. I remember commenting to a born Rhodie that I was a better Rhodesian than he was, because while I was proud to be a Scot, I had become a Rhodesian by choice and not by accident of birth. If only we could turn the clock back. I thank God for my 32 years in a wonderful country.

All my family now reside in South Africa and all are in good positions and now have family responsibilities - we all miss good old Rhodesia and we hate Mugabe's guts.

In 1983 I became a Christian and regret not having a personal relationship with God in my Rhodesian days because I would have appreciated my precious country even more. I would like to return to minister there but am confined to a wheel chair with multiple sclerosis. I do pray for Zimbabwe and believe it can be restored economically and with good rains through revival.

Achieved a reasonably high position in employment. Came to terms with Afrikaans. Became a reasonable bowler and generally I have come to terms with life. I will always treasure the experiences both sad and happy serving in the BSAP reserve and PATU. I might add that for me "This was my finest hour."

What is going to happen when present government is out? What about possibilities of new constitutions discriminating further against white land and gun owners and their religious beliefs.

Since returning to South Africa in 64 my husband taught and lectured for Provincial Administration and eventually became Deputy Director of Education for the province. We hated our first 5 years here but have now settled and are happy. At our return to South Africa husband was amazed to see how far advanced the Rhodesian education system was compared to South Africa but we did not dare say so. We shall always remember our days in Rhodesia as being the best time of our lives and wouldn't have missed the experience for anything.

Questioned at Park Station, Johannesburg as cross border traveller (mistaken identity) 1950. Worked in building industry for 59 years in 4 countries, 3 countries in Africa and United Kingdom. Working in a developing country with untrained persons who work in a "give me" situation who lack responsibility.

Since my pension is now so small I am now employed on a part time basis to supplement my income. We are quite well and happy at present but concerned about the future as we are getting older.

All related in book "Sabotage and Torture". Although Zimbabwe government was well aware of who was responsible for Thornhill sabotage - have never had the guts to come out and apologize for our (6 Air Force officers) arrest - torture - trial - rearrest - detention and deportation. Just this would mean a great deal to all of us now - despite our innocence the stigma remains and I'm often asked "Did you really do it?"

Am happy I moved but would have done better if I left 5 years earlier. My "Old Mutual" pension, was R60-60 last month. Must save for 2 months to go out to supper.

Would return to Rhodesia but not Zimbabwe.

We have both been very lucky in our adopted country in that we have both found excellent jobs and have been able to live at a very high standard. We have not been altogether happy however. We have always felt as if there was something amiss! We miss our country and our people more than words can say.

In Feb 94 I applied to regain my Rhodesian citizenship. I completed and sent the forms with Z$100 to the Dept. of Immigration in Harare but have never had a reply or receipt.

Had I had the same set of circumstances I would have emigrated to Australia between 79-82.

We tried to build a comfortable life for our retirement. Due to devaluation of $Z my pension has been cut by 70%. This has caused considerable worry and belt tightening. After a life time of hard work this outcome is extremely hard to accept. We loved Rhodesia.

Will never regret the 27 happy years spent in a once great country.

In our 19 years in South Africa we own our own large townhouse, have a reasonable income from a pension and medical aid an these grow to cope with inflation. we can travel outside the country and could emigrate if we wanted (but don't). We have always had world class medical treatment available. If we had stayed in Rhodesia we may have enjoyed the same standard of living but would be financial prisoners and not very good medical facilities. Both our sons, born in Rhodesia, are married and doing very well in South Africa.

Developed range of very effective air weapon systems for Rhodesian Air Force. Iraq ordered upgrade of one system. Rhodesians ,who I used in Rhodesia, were in South Africa. I joined them in 83 to develop a system in South Africa and test it in Iraq using Russian aircraft. Very successful and lucrative. Eventually lost all gains. Developed and marketed laser distance-sensor which required no reflector. Economic recession caused mines to ban purchase of any capital equipment. Lost equivalent of R1,2 million. Had to start from zero again.

Despondency about the future of all Africa precludes any constructive thoughts or ideas. What AIDS doesn't get, internecine, inter-tribal warfare and overpopulation will. Will they ever learn?

I left Zimbabwe without regret. Never looked back. My wife had a little trouble settling down. We return to Zimbabwe every year for spiritual renewal and see old friends and family. South Africa has been very good to us. We acquired capital assets of R1 million. We have worked hard and risked investment. I always marvel what 250,000 whites men women and children assisted of course by the blacks achieved. Will history ever record the high level of individual leadership and initiative they possessed.

Found no difficulty apart from monetary ones to establish ourselves in South Africa. Within 3 years we established a company and within 5 years owned our own home, 3 companies and grossed over R2,5 million p.a. Plenty of opportunities, especially in the emerging states for those prepared to take a risk.

Soon after arrival in South Africa along came public holiday. We lived in Verwoedburg- close to Pretoria. In typical Rhodesian fashion we were sprawled in deck chairs soaking up the sun, newspapers spread out, coolie bag full of Castles, ready to brai. Out of every door around came the neighbours in their Sunday best bound for kerk. Pink-crimp dressed women, children and spouses dressed uniformly in dark suits, grey shoes and white ties. All glowered at us. We hadn't realized it was Day of the Vow. Not a good start!

Apart from some weird South Africans I've met here I have also met some weirdos who claim to be Rhodesian but I don't know where they came from actually. I'm very mixed up anyway because although born in Southern Rhodesia I left as a young girl and was educated in northern Rhodesia.

Very hard time after all interest was stopped on my account. Then had to try to live on my anniversary allowance of $Z3000 and my small government pension.

The goodwill and friendliness of all the people made Rhodesia a great place to live and, as we saw on a recent visit, this atmosphere still obtains in Zimbabwe. This could be the main inducement to return to Zimbabwe if life in South Africa becomes too uncertain because, lets face it, there are unknowns there too.

I live and work for Cluny Farm centre which provides a protective working an living environment for intellectually handicapped adults - a rewarding occupation.

My father arrived in Rhodesia in 1904 and is still alive and well. I loved Rhodesia. Even the wogs can't kill the place.

A lifetime in medicine - mainly as specialist obstetrician and gynecologist. 30 years in Rhodesia and 11 in South Africa. Still in part time practice for interest and the money. Regretfully South Africa is going the same way as Rhodesia.

Emigrating was more traumatic than I anticipated. Homesickness was acute at times taking me 4/5 years to settle. After 6 years I realized I was no longer Rhodesian and Rhodesia was no more. I now regard myself as British yet still stateless in a sense. South Africa is definitely no home - just a place to live. Feeling stateless has pros and cons as we feel we could live anywhere and are very adaptable which leaves one with rather too many options.

I would be better off if I could drop medical aid contributions but conditions in provincial hospitals are deteriorating rapidly - quality of attention is falling fast. I have been lucky enough to purchase life rights at a flat belonging to an Anglican church scheme but there are no facilities for frail care. Luckily I enjoy reasonable health and can still drive myself about.

I am back in the same financial position with a house paid for - lovely house and garden and the same maid we took on when arriving. Joburg is really a beautiful city in the suburbs, tree lined, a city one could be very proud of - every activity for everyone living here but a rat race. Was employed initially as a saleswoman, won top prize in South Africa - first class trip to Rio for 2 all paid.

Rhodesians had a bad name in Cape Town in 81. Caused by previously arrived people from Zimbabwe (Rhodesia) who were not too ethical or honest. We were seen as unreliable, riding on the issue of participating in a 16 year war. By 84 the climate had reversed and local employers were employing Rhodesians because they were hard working, reliable and innovative.

Seriously thinking of moving to Canada or Australia due to current situation in South Africa.

I presently sell second hand clothes at flea markets - farms to the black population which I enjoy as I meet a different class of people on different terms. Missed family at first and were very lonely but now have established ourselves and will not go back.

Leaving Zimbabwe for South Africa gave us some years of good education, hospitals etc. but for how much longer I don't know. The worst thing is that had I stayed on in my old job in Zimbabwe I could have retired last year with 31 years service.

Having tried Scotland for 2½ years, England for 2 and been unable to create a warm comfortable place in which to live we gave up the battle and came to the Cape. Family was the specific draw to South Africa. No one should attempt to live in the United Kingdom unless they are loaded and can get away for 8 months each year.

I did my Air Force training at Heany and got my wings there. I loved the people and the country so much that I applied to the Standard Bank for a transfer when I returned from active service overseas. Problem - we ex Rhodesians have tried to get the Zimbabwe government to give us a better tax allowance for old people over 70. The rand/Z$ exchange rate brings us into the highest income tax rate of 55%.

I am concerned that so many loyal, hard working Rhodesians now depend on Zimbabwe pensions. However do they survive if they have no alternative means? I am fortunate to be able to survive.

Despite a struggle when we first got to South Africa we have survived and managed fairly well. We stayed with a relative when we first got to Cape Town and our son wasn't even 2 weeks old when we were told to find accommodation as they were going overseas. We borrowed money for our first flat and after that just never seemed to find our feet financially. Husband's first pay cheque left us with R9 for food after rent, lights, water etc. but generally we are better off than lots of people and have absolutely no regrets about leaving Zimbabwe.

Both my wife and I are very sports oriented - we started badminton clubs, played tennis but are now more into bowls. On various committees, run a bowls tournament in Drakensberg. Chairman of body corporate in complex where we lived and am chief coordinator for 39 neighbourhood watches which I started from scratch. Work fairly closely with South African police.

On a journey home from Umtali to Umvuma at age 11 in charge of the train conductor I was left at Gwelo station waiting room and told to stay with my luggage until called for the connection. Cold and afraid I waited to the early hours of the morning. Reduced to tears, I went out to the platform to ask if it was all right. A soldier in uniform and kit bag asked why I was crying and told me I had missed the train but he was going to Umvuma and would take me. It was my brother Frank returning from France at the end of WW1.

Glad to have joined Rhodesian Forces in 36 and later, Police Reserve.

Many marriages could not stand the upset of emigration. I am considering moving to the United Kingdom because of rapidly deteriorating situation in South Africa.

I am due to take early retirement from my present job in July and will be staying in my own house. Pension from investments in RSA, retirement annuity (RSA) and very small Zimbabwe pension.

My medical aid cancelled my membership in June 87 after 49 years membership because I had been resident in the United Kingdom for over 3 years. This, together with the devaluation of the Z$ causes me great concern for my financial and medical future.

Nothing that has happened in Zimbabwe since independence has been a surprise, except for the speed at which Uncle Bob and his cohorts have brought the economy to its knees. Bless the relatively few whites who keep things running.

My children have excelled at school. My son was head boy both in junior and senior school. Both have good jobs and at least what I set out to achieve when I left, have achieved. We have a lot to be thankful for and I would not move again unless it was to return to Zimbabwe (perhaps) to retire! (This is only a DREAM).

Too many changes to mention have occurred. For a year after leaving Rhodesia I remained quietly arrogant. In the United

Kingdom fiercely and openly patriotic and more recently have a distant fondness, due to my non involvement. I feel bitter in a way that I have been deprived of my heritage - especially for my own daughter who has no knowledge of my birthplace. I look on this as a growth situation and emphasize to my children that nothing is forever and to use whatever culture and country to their advantage in their inner growth.

I attempted to duplicate my Rhodesian life style and to a large extent have done so - rural life in a small town. I am a Zimbabwean/Rhodesian in outlook and remain so proudly.

I find South Africans generally unlike Rhodesians in that they are very cliquey people and very money oriented.

Leaving large computer company in 77 I joined its related company in South Africa as middle manager. In 82 at age 64 I became Company Secretary and was asked to stay on past 65 and retired at 68. When leaving Rhodesia authorities were persuaded to give me retirement settling in allowance so I arrived in South Africa with R12000 plus employment. I now own a duplex on Natal South Coast - I was one of the very lucky ones.

I am taxed quite heavily on my small pension and am trying to find out what benefit I get for what I pay. In Aug. 93 I went to Zimbabwe and at the border was asked for R85 for a visa. When I pointed out I was a pensioner from Zimbabwe and paid taxes as well I was blandly informed that because I held a foreign passport I had to pay

I have 4 children and feel all have benefitted by moving to South Africa where there are so many opportunities for them. I have also benefitted in my work with higher promotions than I would have received in Zimbabwe. We have experienced many strange and peculiar experiences due to peoples actions and inconsistency in their attitudes.

I have always been thankful for the years I spent in wonderful Rhodesia and that my children were educated there to a very high standard both academically and morally. So many changes took place while we were there. Went up in 52 to spy out the land and fell in love with Rhodesia even though we were cut off at Zimbabwe ruins due to floods and low level bridges. Crossed country to Bulawayo, had meal and continued to find Umzingwane river over guard rails- crossed and was first car to get to Beitbridge in a week. Realized how valuable strip roads were. I have wonderful memories of my time in Rhodesia which cannot be taken from me.

Rhodesia is no more but it was all worth it. I wouldn't have missed it for the world. A great country and a wonderful people.

My sons helped my late husband and I to come to South Africa as we were over age. I am now adjusting to single life as a widow. Since coming to South Africa I have received lots of kindness from RASA and an Xmas gift of money from the Christian society in the United Kingdom which was greatly appreciated.

I still have wonderful memories of Rhodesia - I will never forget her. As for the future of any of us anywhere - who knows! Especially when one is older.

Despite homesickness for Zimbabwean family I focus on future in South Africa. We would love to go back but it appears impossible. We moved because we lived in Beitbridge but schooling was so bad we sent the kids to Messina. I'm not sure they would go back to Zimbabwe now so our family would not be together. Maybe we can go back - we'll put in our papers and if it's God's will then it will be.

I came to South Africa for my children's education and mother' health. Mother deceased and children now married and left home. We are now grandparents and Darby and Joan.

Rhodesia was Rhodesia. Zimbabwe is not Rhodesia hence the hesitation to return there to live. The people have changed - more materialistic and plastic. Otherwise a lovely place for holidays.

We have been back in South Africa for 2½ years and I was really sad to leave England where we spent 2½ happy years. My English husband missed the sunshine. Have had our ups and downs since leaving Zimbabwe in 83 (as most people have) and most definitely we shouldn't have moved in the first place.

No real problem - only missing my house.

Worked hard and was able to buy a house in 3 years. Single handedly rewired a Viscount airliner in 8 months. Joined RAF in 1947. First aircraft worked on was DC3. 47 years later in 94 completely rewired a DC3. That must be some kind of record. It was a bit difficult sorting out all that spaghetti wearing bifocals

In my opinion Rhodesians are best suited to adjust to new environment in towns/ cities of the same size they came from. Rhodesians live in new countries but never belong unless they are prepared to stop being Rhodesians.

We should all go back and "take over."

Devaluation of Z$ makes our Zimbabwean annuity and pension worth less than half. This plus inflation causes economic stress on people on fixed incomes.

We can afford and enjoy our retirement but are not sure how long this will continue. We are fortunately in good health and hope this lasts as medical care is so expensive.

Arrived with very little in 79 - worked hard - now retired at sea resort (Ballito) hopefully self sufficient. Tremendous support from wife in all this.

We had a new lady start at our work. At the end of the first day she remarked “You are a Rhodesian aren't you?”. I agreed but asked how she knew. She replied “You are the only friendly, helpful person here - like all the people from Rhodesia”. What a compliment to the Rhodesian nation.

We went to South Africa in 79 and acquired a domicile with favourable exchange rate. The conditions started to deteriorate almost immediately. In 86 we were lucky to get “life rights” in a superior retirement village. We have security, comfort and compatible friends. We had to readjust considerably but have very limited holidays. Get meager assistance from our medical aid in Zimbabwe but heaven help us if we get seriously ill and at our age this is almost certain to happen soon. What happens then?

At first people were sceptical about bush war and felt it could never happen in South Africa. Employers admitted Rhodesians worked harder and achieved more than local staff. Found Rhodesians more willing to look to future of country than many locals, especially those who had never been outside the country.

Main emphasis has been on rebuilding business in South Africa. Part-time military career has been continued.

Hardship brings out best in a person and builds character. We determined to stay after Independence but saw the falling standards in education, especially the arts. Two daughters are studying music. We have adopted 2 Zulu boys and are very happy.

Surviving in spite of Z$ but how long is anyone's guess.

I look back on my years in Rhodesia as the best, happiest and most rewarding of my life. It was the perfect environment in which to bring up my 3 children. I feel I made a small contribution to the future development of the country.

Living in Pretoria I have been very successful having bought and paid for a house in 6 years, retired for a second time after 16 years in a senior position. Still work on freelance basis. Life is certainly different but I am a survivor and make the most of it. I am still proud to be a Rhodesian.

Applied for residence to USA and Canada - wife's aunt tried to sponsor but turned down - too old, not allowed to work and pension considered insufficient - anyway turned out the best for us - South Africa has been good to us.

Overall the memories of a beautiful country, space and Africa are still as strong as ever. Planning to move to South Africa in near future. Possible move back to Zimbabwe if the buggers will give me my residence back.

I sometimes wonder how we Rhodesians misread our black countrymen so badly. We thought they were happy - clearly they were not and showed us so when they got the chance. I know intimidation was rife but we (including myself) totally misread the situation eventually forcing us to leave a country where I spent the best and happiest years of my life and where I planned to grow old with my family now split across half the world.

Whenever financially possible I return to Zimbabwe and often feel homesick for dirt roads during the damp, dreary Irish winter and long for clear blue sky, sunshine and a braai.

I have just finished my book "Quest for freedom" which I started during the bush war. As my country Poland was also continuously fighting for freedom my observations during 30 years of living in Rhodesia was probably different from other Rhodesians.

I don't think I would have been the same person I am today had I stayed in Rhodesia. I am eternally grateful for my childhood there. I will never forget the men and women who spared their lives to make those wonderful years possible. As a Rhodesian in the 90's I have had to refocus on the future while drawing courage from the lessons of the past .....lest we forget!

I would say that 80% of the Rhodesians I have met or heard of in South Africa have "made it". In the main they have improved their lot or maintained it. The other 20% could be classed as "whenwes" who unfortunately have made their mark in South Africa and as a result the name "Rhodesian" is often spoken in a derogatory manner (not at management level).

My 3 children have all achieved responsible positions since moving to South Africa - all attended schools in Bulawayo. Their achievements confirm that education and Rhodesian way of life have equipped them for the future world.

The extreme pressure of living in a foreign land was, in my mind, a cause of me taking the Lord Jesus Christ as my personal savior.

I miss that "special something" that was unique to Rhodesia and will never be recaptured in any country in the world. "Speaking the same language" from RW says it all.

Our 3 children have excelled in academic and career paths. Rhodesians generally have been regarded as dedicated people and most likely to succeed in whatever undertaking they commit themselves to.

We live at MOTH cottages for the last 7½ years and I thank the Lord in Heaven every night for looking after my wife and myself.

Leaving Zimbabwe was the worst decision of my life. It is so special and nowhere else is so special or the people. It's quite unique and wish I could return.

We moved for children's education. Both had good jobs, owned own home, caravan, boat etc. Lived a nice relaxed life style. We hated leaving and would return again but we are too old to start again with nothing much from South Africa. Had great difficulty in settling down in South Africa.

Doing temporary job for Vanderbylpark council in an attempt to boost my ailing Zimbabwe pension. I am still driving my 1961 model Mercedes 180D bought in Rhodesia in 64.

Managed cattle ranches in Rhodesia. Today am mill manager. From 74-94 became experienced in many different kinds of work. Feel secure today and have 10 years to retirement - plan to complete my fishing boat to take customers deep sea fishing as an income during retirement years.

Standing on Thompson's Beach next to brai I said to my husband "That chicken has been on for ages - it's going to be gotcha'ed by the time you finish." Heads swung in all directions at the word "gotcha" and very soon a whole lot of little separate groups became one party of ex Rhodies.

SA has brought material benefits but we have experienced more disasters/misery than we could have ever believed possible - not the country's fault but the way it happened and we are grateful to have permanent residence and our children have obtained very good qualifications - really what more could one want.

After living in Rhodesia where everyone stuck together I find understanding the South Africa preoccupation of keeping up with the Joneses difficult. The "It will never happen to us" mentality sounds ridiculous in view of current situation. They are so busy still fighting the Boer War that I doubt they have even noticed the change.

While living in USA I visited South Carolina. At a restaurant the waitress said I had a "cute" accent and asked where I was from. I replied "Rhodesia." Very blank look on her face "From Africa". She looked really puzzled then asked "Where is that? I don't know of any state called Africa. Is it near California?"

I was very happy living in Zimbabwe but came here to remarry. It didn't work out so I divorced. I still miss Zimbabwe but probably wouldn't return as most of my family are now here. I felt safer and freer while living in Zimbabwe.

Life has been hard in South Africa and we have never retained the status and quality of life achieved in Rhodesia. I retained my business interests and that extra income helped keep us going. I am in the happy position of being able to return to live in Zimbabwe but for tax reasons prefer not to. Their tax rates are ridiculous and there is a 30% capital gains tax which effectively takes your money off you purely because of inflation.

I have the satisfaction of retaining my independence and knowing that my granddaughters include a lab technician, a B. Comm and an architect. My daughter's family includes an Air Force engineer, 2 daughters in highly paid banking positions plus a youngster about to study radiology. Proud attainments in the 15 years since they emigrated. They were all born in Rhodesia.

In my experience those aged 35+ when they left have stayed in a "Wasn't it marvelous then and how I wish I could turn the clock back" instead of grasping new opportunities. I have accepted all that was lost, mourn for it but get on with a new life, new friends and career. I bought my first flat 34 months after arriving, aged 20. I know I wouldn't have achieved this in Zimbabwe. Unfortunately 99% of Rhodies we meet whinge about their misfortune and prey on other's hospitality. It seems a sad image to portray.

The strongest point on my CV is that I'm ex BSAP and ex Rhodesian. This has really opened doors and been a great lever in the competitive job seeking game. I've been in business for some time now and can honestly say that its success is due to Rhodie support.

Since coming to South Africa in 89, 2 of our daughters are now back in Rhodesia. Our third would go but her husband is a Johannesburger and he won't go up there. I'm 72 years old, Scotch by birth, Rhodesian by adoption. Served in RAF during war.

Are you reading a copy borrowed from friends? Need a Christmas or birthday present for a special friend? Want to let the world know how it really was? Need an extra copy for your own archives? Want do some further research yourself? Order an extra copy or a disk of the data or even the full tables.

Name...

Postal Address...

....

....

....

Post Code...................................Country................................

Please enter your name and address above (legibly!). Then complete the order blank overleaf

Payment must be made in either sterling on a UK bank or US $ on a US bank and made payable to InnoVision. UK and US postal orders are acceptable. California purchasers must add relevant sales tax. No credit cards please.

Mail orders to : InnoVision
555 Santa Alicia Dr.
Rohnert Park, CA 94928-3213, USA

Email 72073.1207@compuserve.com.
Phone or fax queries to USA (707) 795-3031. NB: We are 8 hours behind GMT. Remember surface mail may take up to 4 months to reach some countries.

US $ Prices

Copies	Title	Price	Air mail	Surface	Cost
	A Chronicle of Modern Sunlight	14-95	10-00	5-00	
	Full tabular report	25-00	45-00	15-00	
	Data disk of results (IBM format)	5-00	1-00	N/A	
	Total cost				
	Sales tax (California residents only)				
	Total remittance				

Payment must be in US $ on a check, P.O., or draft drawn on a bank in the USA payable to InnoVision

UK £ Prices

Copies	Title	Price	Air mail	Surface	Cost
	A Chronicle of Modern Sunlight	9.95	7.00	3.00	
	Full tabular report	15.00	30.00	10.00	
	Data disk of results (IBM format)	3.00	1.00	N/A	
	Total cost				
	Total remittance				

Payment must be in UK£ on a cheque, P.O. or bank draft drawn on a bank in the United Kingdom payable to InnoVision: InnoVision: 555 Santa Alicia Dr., Rohnert Park, CA 94928-3213, USA

Are you reading a copy borrowed from friends? Need a Christmas or birthday present for a special friend? Want to let the world know how it really was? Need an extra copy for your own archives? Want do some further research yourself? Order an extra copy or a disk of the data or even the full tables.

Name..

Postal Address...

....

....

....

Post Code.....................................Country...................................

Please enter your name and address above (legibly!). Then complete the order blank overleaf

Payment must be made in either sterling on a UK bank or US $ on a US bank and made payable to InnoVision. UK and US postal orders are acceptable. California purchasers must add relevant sales tax. No credit cards please.

Mail orders to : InnoVision
555 Santa Alicia Dr.
Rohnert Park, CA 94928-3213, USA

Email 72073.1207@compuserve.com.
Phone or fax queries to USA (707) 795-3031. NB: We are 8 hours behind GMT. Remember surface mail may take up to 4 months to reach some countries.

US $ Prices

Copies	Title	Price	Air mail	Surface	Cost
	A Chronicle of Modern Sunlight	14-95	10-00	5-00	
	Full tabular report	25-00	45-00	15-00	
	Data disk of results (IBM format)	5-00	1-00	N/A	
	Total cost				
	Sales tax (California residents only)				
	Total remittance				

Payment must be in US $ on a check, P.O., or draft drawn on a bank in the USA payable to InnoVision

UK £ Prices

Copies	Title	Price	Air mail	Surface	Cost
	A Chronicle of Modern Sunlight	9.95	7.00	3.00	
	Full tabular report	15.00	30.00	10.00	
	Data disk of results (IBM format)	3.00	1.00	N/A	
	Total cost				
	Total remittance				

Payment must be in UK £ on a cheque, P.O. or bank draft drawn on a bank in the United Kingdom payable to InnoVision: 555 Santa Alicia Dr., Rohnert Park, CA 94928-3213, USA●